RISING

Stories of the 2013 Alberta Flood

Taylor Lambert

To the people of Alberta;
may we not soon forget
what was lost and gained.

Author's Note

Maps

AUTHOR'S NOTE

THE GREAT FLOOD OF 2013 was a moment in time that will reverberate through Alberta's future for unknown years. The personal, human stories of loss and gain; of devastation and heroism; of stoicism and determination—these are at least in small part glimpsed, I hope, in this book. But the political fallout, the controversy, the anger and resentment towards authorities, the public financial cost—these storylines will play out across years, perhaps generations; thus, they are not closely analyzed in this book.

Albertans are not typically known for being bereft of opinion, and I have no doubt there will be those who will question the makeup of this project: why this, and not that? Why this neighbourhood, and not that one? Why Siksika, and not Stoney or Tsuu T'ina? Why so little on the zoo and the Stampede? Why not more history? Why so much history?

Suffice it to say that I wrote the best book I could under limited circumstances. This book may not satisfy everyone, but it is my sincere hope that it can be appreciated for where it succeeds and forgiven for where it may fall short.

A great deal of thanks is due to those who participated. A book of this nature is an overwhelming task, and reconstructing events from memories requires significant commitment to and belief in the project from both interviewer and subject. The victims, volunteers and others who shared their emotional memories with me deserve more thanks than I can give for their support and patience.

I believe I have done my due diligence as a journalist regarding the personal recollections in this book. Accounts were confirmed and corroborated to the greatest extent reasonably possible; if they seemed unreliable, they were discarded. Human memories are ephemeral by nature, especially with the passage of time. Two people may perceive and recall the same situation differently, much to their own surprise. This is particularly true for those whose memories were formed in emotional or panicked moments.

The length and depth of my questioning was thus often burdensome for those sharing their stories with me as I sought clarification on the tiniest details. Many hours of interviews, many phone calls, many emails, many cups of coffee, meetings in cars, meetings in frigid houses with no heat, clarifications and misrememberings and changes and confirmations—and, after many months of work, you hold the result in your hands.

Not all of the research was done this way, of course, and there is a list of references at the conclusion of the book. However, I have not cited sources for details that were widely reported by all or most news organizations, nor those facts that are very minor or commonly understood. In these instances, citing the hundreds of news articles I consulted would be tedious and redundant. (Sincere thanks to my fellow journalists whose fine work was indispensible when researching these events.)

I have no desire to affix blame or scold any party, group, or government. I refrain from editorializing in these pages. My one hope is that Albertans will not make the mistake of forgetting this event. These stories deserve to become part of our shared memory, not only to honour the spirit of those who suffered, succumbed, and surmounted, but also to remember that though we live in this beautiful environment, we believe ourselves to have tamed it at our peril.

To that point, I end this note with the rather appropriate words of Robert Ingersoll: In nature there are neither rewards nor punishments—there are only consequences.

—Lambert

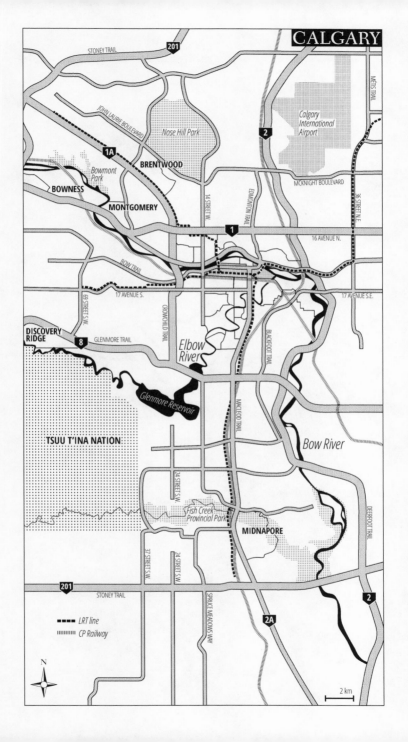

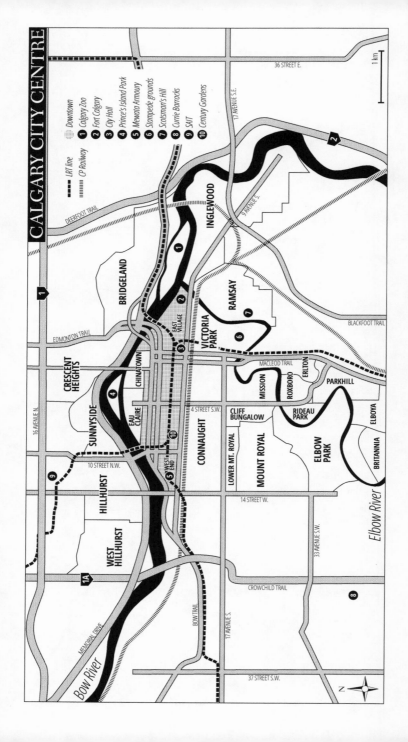

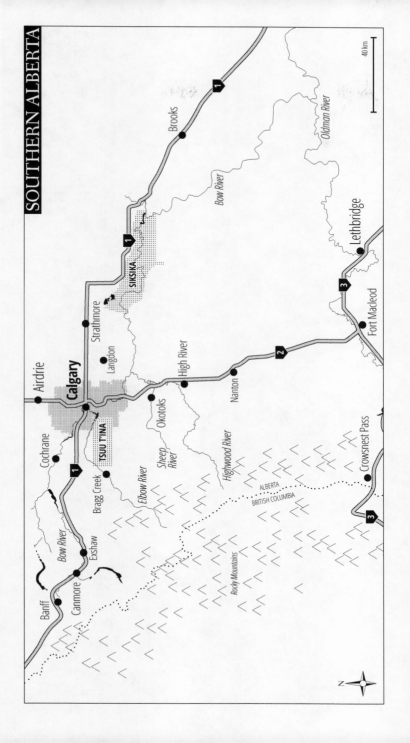

SOUTHERN ALBERTA

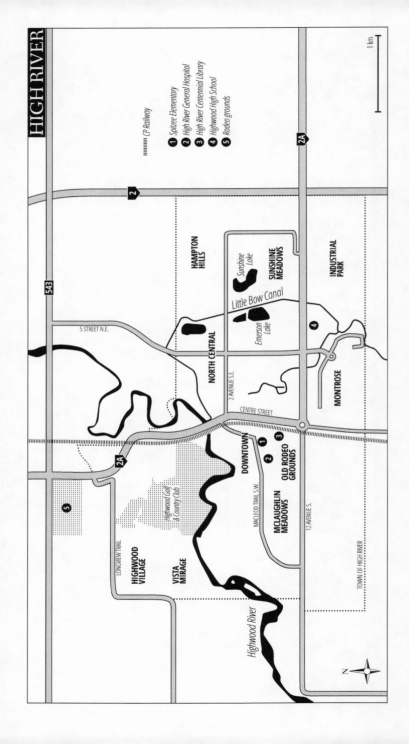

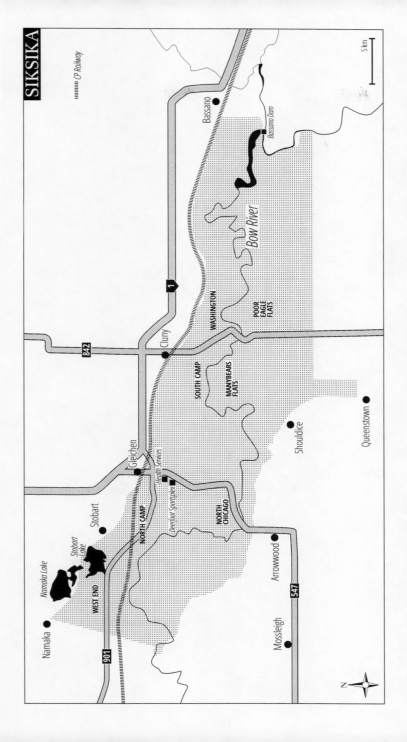

The ripples begin where I begin: they wash up
on that large circle, the world.
 ... the Bow River, the gentle green river which
has always flowed,
flowed longer than the Rockies have stood as
the sentinels of time we believe them to be,
flowed always on the western edge of the small
green world I have always called home.

—Jon Whyte, *Minisniwapta*

Accuse not Nature, she hath done her part;
Do thou but thine.

—John Milton, *Paradise Lost*

A BRIEF HISTORY

Calgary has from its very origins been defined by its waters. Long an important location for the Blackfoot and other indigenous peoples, the confluence of the Bow and Elbow rivers was first settled by the North-West Mounted Police in 1874, one hundred thirty six years after French fur trappers first settled in Winnipeg.

For twenty years, American whisky traders from Montana made annual forays into the area via the Whoop-Up Trail to sell and trade with the aboriginals. But their presence became dangerous to both the security of the region and the well-being of the First Nations, and in the spring of 1875 Parliament passed an order-in-council authorizing construction of a permanent police fort on the Bow, deep in the heart of what was then the Northwest Territories.

Éphrem Brisebois, commander of the NWMP's 'F' Troop, forded the Bow from the north as he returned from Red Deer after receiving the federal order. The first rudimentary fort was built by autumn from logs of spruce and pine cut upstream and floated down the Elbow. Brisebois soon named the post after himself, but was widely regarded as a weak commander whose troops were insubordinate nearly to the point of mutiny; a more suitable name for the fort was needed.

The assistant commissioner of the NWMP, James MacLeod, suggested the name of Calgary, which was the name of a bay on the Isle of Mull in Scotland he had visited years earlier. Colonel A.G. Irvine wrote to the Minister of Justice in Ottawa to pass on this suggestion, "which, I believe in Scotch means 'clear running water,' a very appropriate name, I think." This name was accepted and Fort Brisebois became Fort Calgary. Though clear running water would indeed have been a fine name for a settlement between two rivers, *Cala Ghearraidh* is actually Gaelic for 'beach of the meadow.'

Thus was born the modest settlement of Calgary, created as an act of the federal government. The whisky traders were soon pushed out, but less than a decade later it was apparent that the presence of the fort was doing more to harm the local native population than the whisky trade ever did. The signing of Treaty No. 7 in 1877 had restricted the five First Nations that had inhabited southern Alberta since time immemorial to five reserves, including the Tsuu T'ina to the southwest of Calgary and the Siksika Nation sixty kilometres southeast. The natives who remained had few options but to find an existence within the new economy of the area, providing trade and low-pay services to the other residents of Fort Calgary. Prostitution, begging, and petty theft were common.

The land on the southwest shore of the confluence, where

the fort was situated, was largely reserved for government use. Thus, settlers had built their shacks, houses and businesses on the east shore of the Elbow. This area, named Inglewood in 1911, was the first commercial district of Calgary. But by the late 1870s, the region's bison herd had been decimated and the isolated local economy was faltering. The Hudson's Bay Company considered abandoning its post. Staples were expensive, and there was little money to buy them.

Then, two things ocurred that would forever change the region. First, the federal government removed the import duties on cattle from the United States and introduced a long-term land lease system. The latter of these policies was controversial, but the effect of the two together was transformative. In 1881, the first major herd of cattle was driven through the area en route to Cochrane. More would follow. Southern Alberta became cattle country.

The second key development came soon after when the Canadian Pacific Railway drew their route to the west coast through Calgary. The promise of a link to the cities and markets of the east, and the shipping of the west coast, boosted optimism in the fledging prairie settlement. More than anything before, the railway lent a sense of legitimacy and importance: Calgary would no longer be just another dot on the map.

By the fall of 1883, the railway had reached the far bank of the Bow east of Calgary. Though a location for the station had not been announced, there was an assumption among residents that it would be near the majority of the homes and businesses on the east bank of the Elbow. But after a drawn-out and occasionally controversial attempt to acquire land from various parties, the railway announced that the station would be built west of the existing fort.

The residents' hopes of prosperity as a result of the rail traffic coming through the area were thus dampened. What good were trains if they were two kilometres away?

Tenacious and stubborn—and with a settlement still largely comprised of wooden, non-permanent structures— the people of Calgary pulled many houses, stores, and two churches across the frozen Elbow River on skids to start a new settlement nearer the station, in what is today downtown Calgary. The east bank of the Elbow would be largely abandoned for many years, with only a few residents remaining, including wealthier businessmen who had built brick houses that couldn't be moved so easily.

In 1884, Calgary incorporated as a town. In 1891, the Calgary-Edmonton railway opened. City status came in 1894 after growth had recovered from a dry spell that hurt the agriculture industry. In the early 20th century, there began a strong push to carve new provinces out of the sprawling Northwest Territories, which stretched from the Arctic Ocean to the 49th parallel. The premier of the Territories favoured one large province called Buffalo, with Regina as its capital; Sir Wilfred Laurier, prime minister at the time, feared that such a province could become more powerful than Ontario or Quebec. Proposals such as three provinces, or two with a latitudinal division, were made and ultimately rejected: on September 1, 1905, Alberta and Saskatchewan joined Confederation.

The debate over which Alberta city would gain the legislature and become the capital had long since begun. On January 20, 1905, the *Calgary Herald* ran an editorial predicting that Calgary would be chosen as capital. The following day, the *Edmonton Journal* ran an editorial predicting that Edmonton would be the seat of government. The debate and political manoeuvering that culminated in the 1906 selection of Edmonton were at times acrimonious. Combined with the later debate over the location of the provincial university—which in Saskatchewan had gone to the city that lost the capital, Saskatoon; in Alberta, Edmonton won both—the tension deepened a rivalry and mistrust that would define Alberta politics for generations.

In 1947, a significant oil deposit far bigger than any previously known in Western Canada was discovered at Leduc, south of Edmonton. Oil became the new hot industry in the province, and Calgary was soon reaping the benefits. It was boom time and growth skyrocketed, increasing the population of the city to 181,000 by 1956, a jump of nearly 41 per cent in five years. Suburbs sprang up, echoing the new ideal of prosperity imported from the post-war United States. Calgary would see sustained double-digit growth for the next thirty years. The city began sprouting taller buildings downtown. The Calgary Stampede, long a popular rodeo and festival, began to develop a strong corporate aspect.

The culture of the city changed over decades from a ranching and agriculture mindset to that of the 'blue-eyed sheik' oilmen in business suits.

Whole communities were swallowed up and amalgamated as the city grew: Bowness, Montgomery, Crescent Heights, Forest Lawn and Midnapore were annexed; Rouleauville became Mission, Riverside became Bridgeland. All the while, residential development companies continued expanding the city with low-density communities, many of which bore little distinction from one another. The fast-growing city was less being planned than it was being sold.

There were busts, times of slowed growth or economic slides. Some people lost money, and a few lost great amounts; others were largely unaffected, though there was a general loss of opportunity and employment in the region during these periods. But on the whole, Calgary's star was rising in every way. A professional hockey team arrived in 1980; the Olympics in 1988. The population of Calgary surpassed one million in 2006, just one hundred twenty-two years after residents pulled their homes across the frozen Elbow River.

Calgary in the new millennium was a city beginning to adjust to its newfound clout and importance. The Calgary Region serves as the southern anchor of the Calgary-Edmonton Corridor, one of the four most urbanized areas in Canada. The population of the corridor accounts for three-quarters of Alberta's nearly four million people, 1.4 million of whom reside in the Calgary Region. Two major airports,

Calgary International and Edmonton International—third and fifth busiest in the country, respectively—serve the province, with thirty flights daily between the two metro centres.

Alberta produces seventy per cent of the nation's crude oil, and nearly eighty per cent of its natural gas. Saudi Arabia's proven oil reserves, second-largest in the world, are estimated at 267 billion barrels; Alberta is third with an estimated 173 billion barrels, more than Russia, Libya and Nigeria combined. There is an enormous amount of money in the ground of this province, and the companies that make enormous profits extracting it are found in Calgary. The city is home to more corporate head offices than any Canadian city outside of Toronto, as well as the tallest skyscrapers not on the shores of Lake Ontario.

Most of the top global investment banks have a presence in Calgary: Bank of America, Merrill Lynch, Goldman Sachs, Deutsche Bank, Citigroup, Barclays Capital, and others. More merger and acquisition deals take place in Calgary than any other Canadian city: in 2012, a local economic development agency estimated that the city accounted for three per cent of merger and acquisition deals in the global energy sector, representing twelve per cent of the world's total dollar energy deal volume.

Unlike the traditional seats of wealth and influence in Central Canada, Calgary was bred of new money: young, educated, modern. By the second decade of the 21st century, the city had reached a tipping point of sorts. The size and opportunity of the city attracted not only industry workers but also intellectuals, artists, students, forward-thinking sorts who wanted to harness the opportunity to shape a still-young but affluent city yet to hit its prime. A public art policy was approved by city council. Renowned international architecture firms bid to design new infrastructure and won awards for the results. A new confidence had emerged. The future looked bright for the city astride two rivers.

THE RAIN WAS NEVER CONSTANT. There had been a lot of rain; that much was obvious. In Calgary, only five days in the first half of June were dry. During the remainder of that time a total of 59.4 millimetres fell—six centimetres in fifteen days, hardly enough to warrant a preemptive evacuation.

There were roots of the disaster elsewhere, farther west, up in the mountains. Spring floods in southern Alberta almost always involve the snow melt. There had been a fair amount of snow that year, but for a natural disaster of this magnitude to occur, many stars have to align.

The snow melt had been late. There were still large packs of snow high up in the mountains in early June, which rainfall would quickly melt. The geography of the Rockies and the Foothills causes water to move very rapidly downhill and downstream. The ground had not completely thawed in many areas, leaving it unable to absorb much water. All of this was waiting June 19 when a stormy weather system became unexpectedly trapped over southern Alberta by a high-pressure system and unusual west-blowing winds.

The government weather station near Barrier Lake, not far from the town of Canmore, recorded a cumulative total of 59.8 millimetres of rain in the first eighteen days of June. On June 19, 157 millimetres fell. On June 20, 66.7 millimetres. On June 21, 41.3 millimetres. Barrier Lake recorded 332.2 millimetres of rainfall for the month of June, eighty per cent of which fell in three days. By comparison, 241 millimetres fell the previous June, no more than 36 millimetres on a single day.

On June 19, Environment Canada predicted that portions of the eastern slopes of the Rocky Mountains would receive as much as 150 millimetres of precipitation over the following two days. That night, gauges in some areas indicated that the rain was falling at four times the rate predicted. By one o'clock the following morning, the flow levels of the Highwood River would surpass both the maximum predicted and the peak of the 1995 flood that wreaked havoc on High River, the small town thirty-seven kilometres south of Calgary with a history of flooding.

The data was so incredible it was disbelieved. The province's river forecast division would later say that staff suspected a malfunctioning gauge was responsible for the numbers. Field technologists were mostly unavailable due to a training course scheduled in Kananaskis and the road closures resulting from the weather.

Three degrees of river advisories are routinely issued by the province. In order of increasing severity: High Stream-flow Advisory; Flood Watch; Flood Warning. The first flood warning was issued at a quarter to seven Thursday morning for the Sheep River, which runs through the town of Okotoks between Calgary and High River. The Highwood River and the Elbow upstream of the Glenmore Dam remained at a flood watch level. Two hours later, those rivers were upgraded to a flood warning, along with tributaries of the Bow River upstream of Calgary.

Cougar Creek is one of those tributaries, a small waterway that flows through the south side of Canmore—where a suburban community called Cougar Creek has been built around it—and joins with the Bow River after crossing under highways 1 and 1A. The rain and rapid snow melt turned the creek into a dangerous torrent, growing many times larger and more powerful. The water ripped apart the landscape and devastated homes. Trees and boulders sped down the mountain causing great damage as they smashed into houses.

After this came Exshaw, a hamlet in the municipal district of Bighorn. The tiny community sits on the north shore of the Bow River downstream from Canmore, just past Lac Des Arcs. Metres of water swamped the streets. Cars were flooded up to their windshields. Buildings near the swollen, powerful river were ripped away.

All of this came hours before Calgary, which receives the Bow from the northwest and the Elbow via the picturesque

Glenmore Reservoir in the southwest quadrant of the city. The Bow winds its way past the formerly independent communities of Bowness and Montgomery into the inner city, along Hillhurst and Sunnyside, past Eau Claire and the Downtown East Village to Fort Calgary and Inglewood. The Elbow, much smaller than the Bow, cuts a narrow and tortuous path eastward and northward, running past some of the most expensive homes on some of the most valuable residential real estate in Western Canada. It delineates the southern and eastern borders of the Stampede grounds before joining the Bow between Fort Calgary and Inglewood.

Both of these waterways would wreak havoc on the city of 1.2 million—the most populous city in Alberta, third in Canada, covering more area than either Toronto or New York. The warnings and predictions were all quite mild. Alberta Environment did not issue a flood warning for either the Bow or Elbow Rivers in the city until a quarter to one Thursday afternoon. Meanwhile, the 2005 flood was the benchmark in the public's mind: nothing could be worse than that; nothing could have indicated river levels five to ten times above the normal flow rates.

The town of High River declared a local state of emergency at five past seven that morning. But High River often had seasonal floods in its low-lying areas. Most people took this for granted. Most people went about their day on June 20 like it was any ordinary Thursday morning.

THURSDAY

Florence and Ken began the day together with a typical breakfast: for Florence, some dry cereal and half a banana; Ken had toast and corn flakes. It was raining, and Florence asked her son if he would take a cheque to the bank for a bill payment so she wouldn't have to go out. Ken agreed.

It had been eleven years since Ken moved back to High River. Tired of fighting with roommates in Calgary, tired of driving down to help his elderly mother with yardwork and house chores, he returned to the family home and found a job selling automotive parts. Seven years later, Ken would be diagnosed with kidney cancer. Eventually, the cancer would metastasize and spread to his lungs and bones. At fifty-seven, Ken had become a large, hunched man who moved about slowly as he got ready to deliver his mother's cheque.

Florence wrote out the cheque. The middle of eleven surviving children born to a Pennsylvanian father and Iowan mother who had met in High River, she had spent her entire life in or around the small town.

Her family had lived on a farm along 7th Avenue Southeast. The Little Bow River ran through their pasture land.

It was a simple, happy life centred on family and church and hard work on the land. Florence loved to skate on the farm's frozen pond in the winter. As a teenager she worked at a creamery, and as an egg grader.

In 1954, Florence married her husband Lyle, the only child of local farmers. The newlyweds lived on land owned by a retiree who was moving to Calgary, and their herd of seven ewes grew to three hundred during the ten years they lived there. Lyle was a quiet, gentle man, and he made a natural shepherd. Three children were born to them during this time: Kenneth, Patricia and Lucinda.

In February of 1964, Florence and Lyle began building a house in High River on 3rd Street Southwest. The modest bungalow was designed and built almost entirely by Lyle, paid for without a bank loan or mortgage. His father-in-law advised him not to move in until it was completely finished: otherwise, he said, it'll never be done. Lyle built it carefully, cutting no corners, and the family moved in on Christmas Eve that same year. Lyle and Florence called it their Christmas and anniversary gifts to each other.

The house was well-situated, close to the school, the downtown, and the hospital. Most importantly, it was well-built: Lyle was the sort of man who overbuilt to support twice the weight, just in case. Only the very best house would do for his young family.

While still living on the farm, Lyle had bought Florence a piano. It was in disrepair, but he lovingly refinished it and had a new keyboard installed. When they moved to the new house, to their dismay, they found it wouldn't go down the stairs to the basement. Lyle solved the problem by removing several ground-level blocks from the basement wall, lying the piano flat on its back, and sliding it into the basement—a feat he accomplished entirely on his own.

For the next thirty-four years, the house was the stage upon which the family's story played out. Family gatherings, birthdays, anniversaries, scraped knees, first dates and graduations; thirty-four years of children and grandchildren, of growing up and moving out.

On Christmas Eve, 1998, Lyle passed away, thirty-four years to the day after he proudly moved his family into their new home. The man was gone, but his house remained, and his widow kept his memory alive inside it. Four years later, Ken moved back in. Eleven years after that, on June 20, 2013, as Florence wrote out a cheque for her son to take to the bank, her house would be tested as never before.

IT WAS HARD TO BELIEVE. But there it was, right in front of him. Jeremy had dropped off his eldest daughter, Hanna, at her preschool on the west side of High River around nine o'clock that morning. He'd made the ten minute cross-town drive back home afterwards. His wife Lani was home, recently laid off from her job as an underwriter. Jeremy, too, had taken some time off from his construction job, and they had plans to use the opportunity to do something together, perhaps take a vacation.

That small but pleasant dream began to unravel as soon as Jeremy returned home. The school is flooded, said Lani, they're evacuating the kids. A friend of Lani's, whose daughter attended the same preschool, had posted this online. Shortly after, the school sent out an email confirming the evacuation; there was no phone call as Jeremy and Lani had yet to give the school their new cell phone numbers.

It all happened so fast: they took their youngest daughter, Mya, and drove back to the school. They parked half a block away—which was as close as they could drive—and got out to survey the scene.

It was hard to believe. But there it was: a small lake stood between them and the school. Cars were stalled and abandoned in the parking lot. Everything had been perfectly normal when Jeremy dropped Hanna off at nine o'clock; it was now a quarter to ten.

Jeremy began walking into the water. He had come prepared with rubber boots, but he was quickly submerged up to his waist. He struggled to keep his footing on the fallen trees and other debris beneath the muddy water. As he walked, he was struck by a thought that scared him: I'm going to be carrying my daughter out through the water. This is real.

But when he reached the school, he found only two other parents who had also waded through the flood waters. They told him the children had already been evacuated to the supermarket a short distance away. The school itself was slightly higher than the rest of the surrounding area, and it had not yet flooded inside. Jeremy and the two other parents decided to leave a note for any other who might come looking for their children. They walked through the school, searching for paper and tape, and Jeremy felt a little bad about leaving muddy bootprints everywhere; he assumed it would only be a matter of hours before everyone returned.

There were only eight children still outside the supermarket when they arrived to pick up Hanna. The two teachers were stressed by the ordeal, but the kids were happily running around, playful and oblivious to what was happening. Their family safely reunited, Jeremy and Lani headed back home.

Though dramatic, none of this was out of the ordinary in the context of a predicted flood. This was, after all, High River, and in their three years as residents, Jeremy and Lani had heard of the floods that preceded their arrival. Some years were worse than others, but water on the street in the notoriously flood-prone old part of town was no reason to call in the army. Their own neighbourhood—a quiet suburban development on the east side—was safely away from the river; there was no chance it could flood, and the thought never ocurred to them.

KEN WENT OUTSIDE TO HIS VAN, which was parked in the rear of the house. The backyard faced west and was bordered by an alley, across which was the large grass field of Spitzee Elementary. There was a great deal of traffic in the alley; cars and trucks went by one after another. People often used the alley as a shortcut, but the number of vehicles struck Ken as odd. He would have to back his van out into the alley to go to the bank, and he decided not to bother for the moment.

Ken went back into the house. I'm not going anywhere right now, he said to his mother. There's too many cars in the alley. It was about half past nine—too late for parents to be dropping children off at school, they reasoned.

Florence went to the east window, at the front of the house. She called her son to come look: cars and trucks were lined up here as well, and the gutters on both sides of the street were overflowing with steady streams of water.

Look at that! said Florence.

Well, they said there'd be a flood of some sort, mused Ken. I suppose I ought to check the basement. And I'll turn off that space heater, too.

You mean you haven't turned that off yet? It's nearly July!

Ken made his way to the basement, lumbering down the stairs in no particular hurry. He shut off the small gas heater that warmed the basement in cooler months. He checked the corner that usually saw some water during the spring thaw (the basement walls were cement blocks, not poured concrete), and there was indeed a small pool of clear water; nothing to be especially concerned about.

Ken checked the downstairs bathroom and found dark-coloured water coming up in the toilet bowl and shower drain. This was more worrisome, and he went back upstairs to tell Florence.

What should we do? she asked. I don't know, said Ken, I guess we'll just keep an eye on it to see if it gets any worse.

Florence walked to the windows to survey the scene in the neighbourhood. To the east, the street in front of the house was still clogged with pickup trucks, and a car had stalled, worsening the situation. The gutters were still full of flowing water. She walked to the west window, where her son was standing. Looking out at the flat, open schoolyard, they both saw it at the same time: a foot of water moved from south to north like a wave over the entire field, faster than a young child might be able to run.

It was a frightening sight. The schoolyard was quickly flooded. The grade of the alley was about one foot higher than the field, and the water was now level with it. Within minutes it was spilling over the alley and filling their backyard. It didn't take long for the water to reach the bottom of the doors on Ken's van. A snowmobile, dirt bike, and riding mower in the backyard were all well into the water. They knew driving their own vehicles was no longer a viable escape plan.

Ken tried calling Aunt Evelyn, who lived in town near the water tower, but the phone seemed to be dead. I think we ought to figure out how to get out of here, he said. The phone lines are down.

Florence heard her son speaking from the kitchen; she was in the south part of the house looking out the window. In the driveway sat her 1997 Chrysler that Lyle had bought for her shortly before his passing.

The tremor and sound waves struck them at almost the same instant. It sounded like a truck had hit the house; it felt like an earthquake. The whole house shook violently. What was that? said Florence after a few moments of shock. Ken went to the front door and saw one of his neighbours from across the street coming towards the house. He told Ken: Your basement wall just collapsed.

The water outside had built up enough pressure on the basement wall to burst through two rows of concrete blocks, as well as the studding and drywall behind it. Florence had been standing nearly directly above the explosion.

Get out of there, Mom! Ken yelled as he rushed downstairs. Water was pouring in from the hole, and the basement was quickly filling. They would have to leave the house, but he had the presence of mind to think of shutting off the gas first. He waded into the water, which was already up to his waist, and made his way across the basement to where the gas control and electrical panel were located. Ken only made it halfway before realizing the danger in what he was doing. The deep freeze was floating in the water, still plugged in. The water was dirty and had a bad smell.

Meanwhile, upstairs, a middle-aged woman had come to the door. You've got to get out now! she told Florence. My son's in the basement, she replied. The woman came in and yelled at Ken to come up. He abandoned his plan and hastily retreated to the staircase.

The woman was a stranger who had taken a walk through the neighbourhood when her office building had flooded, looking to help wherever needed. Ken came upstairs with his jogging pants soaked through and said he needed to change before leaving. I'll go find a truck, said the woman, and she went out into the flooded street to wave down two young men in a pickup. They backed up to the front of the house and Florence and Ken got in. The truck pushed slowly through the water in the street as they drove away from the house Lyle built: broken, filling with water, abandoned to the forces of nature.

———————————

THOUGH SAFE ON THE OTHER SIDE of High River, the flood did colour Jeremy and Lani's afternoon. The town had asked residents to conserve water and reduce the strain on the sewer systems. Soon, friends in other parts of town were evacuated as the flooding spread, and Jeremy and Lani began offering their home as a shelter.

Their friend Jenifer showed up around noon with her dog. Her house had been flooded while she was at work, and her dog had to be rescued by utility workers. Her two young daughters had been evacuated from school and taken by her husband to his parents' house, which was now itself cut off by the water. All she could do was wait to hear where she could pick them up once they were evacuated. Jenifer asked Lani to watch her dog while she went back to work briefly; Lani agreed, and said Jenifer and Ryan and their girls would be welcome to stay with them.

Shortly after Jenifer returned from work, she received a call: her family was being evacuated and she was to pick them up from the relief centre at the high school. It wasn't a long drive—no two points in High River are particularly far apart—but by the time she arrived, the evacuation centre at the high school was itself being evacuated. She collected her husband and daughters and drove back to the safety of Lani's house.

Siksika Nation is the second-largest First Nation reserve by area in Canada. Roughly an hour's drive southeast of Calgary on the Trans-Canada Highway, the sprawling reserve rivals the size of the city proper, though with one quarter of one per cent of the population. The land is typical of southern Alberta: treeless prairie, rolling hills and lush river valleys. The Bow flows tortuously through Siksika from west to east, twisting and turning before emptying into a reservoir above Bassano Dam and then continuing below it.

The Siksika are members of the Blackfoot confederacy, an alliance of four bands—three in Canada, one in the United States—with shared cultural and linguistic roots. The Siksika people number approximately six thousand, half of whom live on the reserve.

At any given time, there are four firefighters on duty at Siksika. The emergency services department is housed in the Health Services building, which sits up on a hill near the intersection of highways 547 and 901. Inside the emergency services section, down the stairs from the offices and reception, are the modest creature comforts afforded to firefighters: a break room and kitchen with a never-ending pot of coffee, comfortable couches and a big-screen television with video game consoles. It was here that Sohkes was waiting, killing time on his shift Thursday morning, when he got toned out.

The alarm tone used to raise firefighters is a sort of loud whistle. It is unmistakeable, impossible to ignore. It is the sound of urgency, the sound of an emergency. It represents both a meaningless, routine false alarm, and total disaster with lives hanging in the balance. It could require simply showing up in a uniform, or it could demand any of the elite skills that set emergency workers apart. It is the sound of a job to be done.

For Sohkes and his partner Lee, the job was a river rescue: a home near the Bow had become surrounded on all sides by the rising waters, and the man inside was trapped. The fire-fighters received their orders and drove down to the site with their rescue boat.

Sohkes—pronounced soo-kee—had spent most of his four years as a firefighter on the reserve. He'd grown up in Redwood Meadows, a townsite on land leased from the Tsuu T'ina First Nation, on the southwest border of Calgary. He'd wanted to be a firefighter for as long as he could remember. His parents and sisters were all educated, professional sorts: lawyers, professors, teachers. But Sohkes wanted more danger and excitement; he wanted to help people in a direct and tangible manner.

His partner Lee was the more senior of the two, a veteran fireman who'd seen a lot and paid his dues. To Sohkes, Lee was a man's man: tough, courageous, never one to show fear or shrink from a situation. Sohkes admired and respected him.

They arrived at the rescue location and saw the task that awaited them. The house was a log cabin that now stood surrounded by the swollen river, which was not only high but extremely fast. Sohkes had done river rescues before—he had specific training for swift water rescues—but the dangerous challenge before him made him uneasy. And then Lee, his fearless and experienced partner, said: Fuck no, we'll get killed!

Their boat was a Zodiac, designed to traverse the river in

its normal state; it was doubtful whether it could contend with the powerful current that rushed around the house where the man was trapped. It was entirely possible that they could capsize or be swept away if something went wrong. Neither Sohkes nor Lee relished the risk involved. But any considerations they may have had for saving their hides quickly gave way to saving face once they saw the media gathered nearby. Ah, shit, they're watching us. Time to get to it.

Under the watchful eye of the press, they prepared the boat. The rather modest motor struggled against the current as they set out for the house. Sohkes noticed the smell of the water: a nauseating odour of gasoline and sewage, picked up by the river as it flooded communities upstream. He put the stench out of his mind and focused on the task at hand.

By aiming against the current enough to slow their drift downstream, Sohkes and Lee managed to reach the house safely. Sohkes jumped onto the porch, which was already underwater. He made his way to the door and tried to open it, but the water in front of the door blocked it, and it required some force to open. Inside, he found their rescuee: an elderly man standing and waiting. He seemed fairly calm considering his house was now in the middle of a river.

Sohkes called to him, but the man replied, No, I think I'll stay. Sohkes tried to keep his patience: You can't stay, sir, your house is going to be washed away soon. What he thought, but did not say: I just risked my life to get to this house, and you're coming with me, old man.

Can I bring my dog?

Yes, yes, get your dog, let's go! The house was old and not particularly sturdy, and Sohkes did not want to linger more than was necessary. He helped the man and his dog into the boat and Lee steered them all back to shore.

The media was indeed watching: the next edition of the *Strathmore Times* featured a heroic-looking Sohkes in the boat with the rescued man and his dog, holding an oar poised mid-stroke with a determined look on his face; Lee, meanwhile, was in the rear of the boat and couldn't be seen at all.

BOW CRESCENT, CONTRARY TO ITS NAME, is a long, mostly straight road in Bowness that runs along the Bow River. Some of the nicest homes in the district are found here, many of them dating prior to 1963, the year that the town of Bowness was swallowed by its ever-growing, land-hungry neighbour and made into part of Calgary.

Ritch and Cathy's house, where they lived with their teenage son and a daughter in her early twenties, sits on a riverfront lot that was long ago subdivided into thirds; theirs is the section farthest from the river. The 2005 flood touched the other two homes on the lot—both large, expensive, modern dwellings—but spared their modest, ageing, beige bungalow hidden behind mature trees.

There was no anticipation late Thursday afternoon, no fear, no cause for concern. The river was high, but spring floods are not uncommon in Calgary, and the water had never made it as far as Ritch and Cathy's house. It was a pleasant twenty degrees outside, and the rain clouds had cleared away, so Cathy took their dog Maggie for a walk.

Across the river from the eastern tip of Bowness, adjacent to the neighbourhoods of Varsity and Montgomery, lies Bowmont Natural Park. Stretching from the lower riverbank up to the grassy open areas high up on the cliffs that hem in the river, the park's very name—a combination of Bowness and Montgomery—indicates its deep roots in the area. Cathy often took Maggie here for walks, and it was here they went that afternoon. Even though the day gave every indication of being ordinary, something compelled Ritch to call out to his wife as she left.

Stay away from the river.

I will.

The river was indeed high near the park, and Cathy stayed well back of it on the trail. Maggie wandered about without a leash, and together they walked up a slight hill where Cathy pulled out a camera she had brought along. She took a few shots of the park and the river from this vantage point, paying no mind to Maggie, who was sniffing about. Cathy reviewed her pictures on the camera's screen and the jingle of Maggie's collar sounded as she approached her owner from behind. Cathy looked down and saw the dog was soaking wet.

Maggie, where did you— Cathy stopped as she saw the path they had come along had been swallowed by the rising river. In a matter of moments, their small hill had become cut off by the water.

Cathy felt panic rising inside her. What do I do now? They were all but trapped. She considered making a push through the water to the dry, higher portion of the path.

No, you can't do that, she thought. Remember that gal who got swept away in the 2005 flood. Cathy turned round to examine their options for escape. As though in response, a deer suddenly emerged from the bushes and darted up the steep hill that led away from the river. Okay, Maggie, we've gotta go. She followed the deer, and Maggie followed her.

The terrain was steep and slippery: both dog and deer fared better than woman as they moved upwards to safety. Soon the deer had gone, and Cathy and Maggie made their way back home.

Her sister Frankie had stopped by the house to drop off some sausages, and Cathy related the story to her and Ritch. They all marvelled at how quickly the river was rising. As Frankie left, they noticed water had appeared on Bowbank Crescent, the small street that ran beside them. It seemed fairly minor and far back from the house, so they all agreed there was no cause for concern.

Fifteen minutes later, Cathy noticed water running down Bow Crescent and realized they were in trouble. It was time to pack.

THE CITY OF CALGARY DECLARED a state of local emergency at a quarter past ten Thursday morning. With Mayor Naheed Nenshi in Ontario on a speaking junket, the decision was taken by Deputy Mayor Richard Pootmans and Alderman John Mar in accordance with the Alberta Emergency Management Act and city bylaw 25M2002.

The city's Municipal Emergency Plan details the response phases with a colourful graph. Moving along the x-axis timeline, we have 'business as usual' until an 'event' strikes; this coincides with a 'business interruption'. Further down the timeline, we have 'business resumption', and getting from interruption to resumption involves three phases with differing levels of time and effort.

First comes 'response', a phase of comparatively short time but maximum effort. During this phase, the emphasis is on minimizing loss of life and impact on the affected area. As the effort level of this phase begins to fall, the second phase rises up to take its place. 'Local authority recovery' is less effort-intensive as the most immediate aspects of the disaster have now passed. The emphasis here is on communication, social services and support networks, and assessment of damage. This phase is longer-lasting on the timeline than the initial response; as it falls off, the third and final phase hits its peak: 'community restoration and rehabilitation.' This is the long-term post-disaster effort, focusing on environmental and economic recovery. By this point, we have reached our goal of 'business resumption.'

This is the plan. This is the guiding document the City will follow in any crisis, emergency, or disaster. But any game plan requires skilled, well-coached players to be effectively implemented.

The Calgary Emergency Management Agency, or CEMA, is an organization rarely heard or seen until called into action. Comprised of directors and senior managers from both City business units and external partners—the province, the military, and so forth—its headquarters are set high above the river in the long-annexed community of Crescent Heights, which takes its name from the semicircular bluffs from which it overlooks downtown. This is the Emergency Operations Centre, a $45 million state-of-the-art building with many rooms equipped for meeting, sleeping, and eating.

Its heart is the ops centre, a huge bunker several metres below ground filled with communications equipment and television screens and computers. In the event of a declaration of a state of local emergency, the top decision-makers congregate here to collaborate quickly and effectively in response to the crisis. Everyone who might be needed is in one place. Several won't leave for days.

The director of CEMA is Bruce Burrell, normally the city's fire chief. On Thursday morning, Burrell joined the rest of the city's leadership at the EOC; Nenshi would cut his eastern tour short and soon join them. The full brunt of the disaster had yet to hit the city, but it was clearly going to be far worse than predicted, worse even than the flood of 2005.

THE YOUNG MEN WITH THE TRUCK drove away from Florence's house down 9th Avenue towards the High River library. But the intersection of 9th Avenue and 1st Street Southwest was deeply flooded, so they retreated and turned down 4th Street, making their way through the residential area to 12th Avenue, which runs along the southern edge of High River and offers spectacular views of the open prairie.

The group was heading for the home of Ken's friend Stu, where Ken and Florence could make some phone calls and check on Aunt Evelyn, who lived in the area. But 12th Avenue was also under water near the Little Bow, so they turned into Montrose, a planned residential community, and wound their way to 5th Street, where they were able to drive all the way north to 4th Avenue and reach the house.

Meanwhile, Florence's granddaughter Alanna was at the school where she taught Kindergarten in the hamlet of Langdon, just east of Calgary. It was graduation day for the youngsters; her morning class had already gone home, and she was helping rehearse with the afternoon class. It was around noon when her mother called her.

Alanna had heard about the flood hitting Canmore and

High River, but it didn't strike her as serious. High River's regular floods never reached the family home even at their worst. The story from her mother Lucinda, then, was quite a shock: her grandmother's basement wall had collapsed from the water, and she and Uncle Ken had had to flee. Lucinda didn't know much else, including where they had gone. But since Alanna was the closest family member to High River—her mother lived in Rocky Mountain House, and Florence's other daughter Pat was in Crowsnest Pass— she ought to start driving there. I'll keep trying to find out where they are, and I'll call you, said her mother.

Alanna immediately went and told her principal she had to leave. Being graduation day, Alanna had worn a dress, which was not conducive to an emergency flood rescue. She traded clothes with another teacher, swapping her dress for jeans; others gave her boots and jackets for herself and her relatives. No one really knew what the situation would be like. Alanna got in her car and began driving south.

The highways were still open, with little apparent evidence of flooding. She kept the radio tuned to the emergency broadcast station, and she heard that the evacuation centre for the town had been set up at the high school. Since she still hadn't heard from her mother about Florence and Ken's whereabouts, she decided to head there.

Once in the town, the flooding was more apparent alongside the roadways, which had unusually heavy traffic for a Thursday afternoon. People were trying to get out, while she was trying to get in.

When Alanna arrived at the high school, she found it filled with people. It was chaos: hundreds of evacuees milled around while relatives searched through the crowd for their loved ones. Officials at a reception desk were keeping track of names, but her grandmother and uncle hadn't registered. She walked through the crowd, looking for them, checking back with the desk after a while. They weren't there.

Finally, her mother called and gave her an address: they were staying with a friend of Ken's. Alanna drove over and found her grandmother in surprisingly good spirits, considering the situation. Ken, however, appeared more troubled; perhaps he grasped the seriousness of the situation more fully.

A plan was made: Alanna would take Florence to her home in Calgary, while Ken would find his own accommodations.

In the chaos of fleeing the house, there had been no time for Florence to think of things like pill bottles. Before leaving the town, Alanna took her grandmother to a pharmacy so she could get her prescriptions refilled. Florence did have a list of her medications, but not the actual prescriptions. Fortunately, the pharmacy staff seemed to be understanding with the many people who had come for much the same reason.

There was a two-hour wait estimated, so they sat and waited. People came in asking for all sorts of things; one person needed insulin for several diabetics at the evacuation centre. After half an hour, someone came in and said the evacuation centre at the high school had been evacuated. The town was beginning to shut down as the water's grip tightened. Alanna called her mother for advice. She told her daughter to leave immediately, before the highways closed.

They headed north towards the city. Alanna and her husband lived in Rosscarrock, in the southwest quadrant. Florence stayed there for five or six hours before Alanna's mother came down from Rocky Mountain House to pick her up and take her to stay there for the time being.

WHILE IN THEIR COMPANY, the man Sohkes and Lee rescued from his flooded house told them that, in the more than sixty years he'd lived on the reserve, this was the worst he'd ever seen the river. Nothing in his memory even came close. The firefighters passed this information to their boss Tom, who took it very seriously.

Tom grew up in Hobbema, today called Maskwacis, a tiny community south of Edmonton that straddles the borders between the Ermineskin Cree Nation reserve, Samson Cree Nation reserve, and Ponoka County. He joined the Muskwachees Fire Department there and began working his way up. He became deputy chief of the department before contracting his expertise out to Indian and Northern Affairs Canada as an inspector and evaluator of fire departments.

He loved his line of work, and he was good at it, and Tom reached the rank of fire chief at Muskwachees before heading south to Siksika to fill the same role there.

Within three years of his arrival, he was handed several more responsibilities including ambulances, medical transport, family violence response, and the crisis unit. All these he carried in addition to his role as fire chief. Economics necessitated the consolidation, but there was also practical sense in streamlining the organizational structure.

Tom had now been director of emergency services for eleven years. As the reserve's point man for heading off and coping with disaster, he was not ignorant of the impending flood. He had known for days that there was something coming: a similar sized flood to 2005 from the sounds of the expert and government predictions. Tom had already ordered the sandbagging of target homes in low-lying areas that had seen flooding that year.

But when he heard of the rescued man's warning about the river, Tom couldn't dismiss it. It was at that point on Thursday afternoon that he began to pay much closer attention to what was happening in Calgary.

AT TWO O'CLOCK THURSDAY AFTERNOON, a conference call was held between Calgary Zoo personnel and their representative at the emergency ops centre. Being partially situated on St. George's Island, just northeast of downtown, the zoo has been vulnerable to flooding since it was first founded: the flood of 1929 covered the island with two feet of water, forcing animal evacuations and causing damage to the roads and gardens.

After more significant flooding in 1932, the first dike was completed on the island in 1935. Others would follow, and these measures saved the island from the level of devastation incurred in its first year. During the 2005 flood, the dikes were supplemented with sandbagging, and only minimal water damage hit the zoo.

Until Thursday afternoon, senior zoo staff foresaw nothing more than perhaps a few centimetres of water in some areas. When their representative at the emergency ops centre told them that the new river flow data suggested most of the island would soon be underwater, it shocked everyone in the room. For people whose lives revolved around the care of animals, it was devastating news.

The floods of the past had not deterred the zoo from extensively developing St. George's Island. Though only about half of the zoo was built in the middle of the Bow River, the island was home to some of the most challenging animals to handle: gorillas, hippopotamuses, giraffes, elephants, lions, snow leopards and tigers. The second-largest zoo in Canada was facing unprecedented disaster and there were only a few hours to act.

JEREMY WENT OUT TO buy groceries to feed the extra mouths in their home. Then he took his bicycle out to see the flooded areas of High River first-hand. The roads were busy with police, work vehicles, evacuees leaving town, and spectators, all in addition to ordinary traffic. Some areas were impassible, others were blockaded, but what he was able to see was incredible: water spilling onto streets and through parks as the level of the Highwood River continued to rise. He went all over town on several bike rides throughout the day, watching the water break into different neighbourhoods.

Jeremy brought along a video camera and recorded footage of the flood. He was an electronic hobbyist who liked experimenting with circuit designs and posting video of the results online, where he had gained a small following. In one video made that day, he shows his viewers the height of the water; marvelling at its power, he then displays a diagram of his latest circuit and jokes: I posted a video last night, but this one is a bit more exciting! The flood was real, and it was serious, and he saw this; but it was still on the periphery of his world, close enough to see, too distant to touch him.

Even during his final bike ride around six o'clock, when Jeremy stood in the stream that was quickly filling the lake near his house and looked back at his corner lot—lower than his neighbours due to the drainage slope—when he finally realized that they were likely to get some water, he did not panic. He went home and barbecued chicken for his family and guests.

After being evacuated from two homes, a school and an evacuation centre, Jenifer and Ryan were glad to have a safe haven. The two families barbecued together and prepared extra beds. The talk was largely of the flood, of course, but Lani tried to stay upbeat and keep her friends' spirits up as much as possible.

But the more Jeremy thought about what he'd seen, the more he began to worry. I think we could get some water here, he told Lani. It looks pretty bad in other parts of town. They might even evacuate us at some point as a precaution.

Oh, don't be silly! We're far away from everything, we'll be fine.

Maybe we should pack some bags. Just in case.

Some preparations were made, and bags were packed. It was a hard reality to swallow, despite the worsening signs around them. Their area of town was considered so safe that residents flooded elsewhere in High River often sought refuge with family and friends there, as Jenifer and Ryan had done. Jeremy's suggestion that the water might reach them was limited to an expectation of a foot or so in the basement in the worst-case scenario, and even that was hard to believe. They were not prepared for the reality that lay ahead.

WITH THE WATER NOW FLOWING down Bow Crescent, Cathy went downstairs and began grabbing whatever she could from the basement to bring upstairs to safety. Her daughter Katie was in her basement bedroom, and Cathy told her to get moving. But Katie couldn't or wouldn't believe it. She refused; she said she was busy packing for her move out of the house that weekend; she pointed out that they moved everything before the 2005 flood, only to be spared any damage. Cathy yelled at her daughter in frustration, but Katie placed a large armchair in front of her door to end the conversation.

The sight of water on their street had put Cathy in a state of panic. She frantically tried to think of what to move up from the basement. She grabbed a few things, then paused to look at a photograph of her late brother and his wife hanging on the wall at eye level.

It's not going to get that high, is it John? Cathy looked at the picture for a moment before moving on. She grabbed some photo albums and headed upstairs, pausing halfway up to grab the clothes iron. She would revisit that moment over and over in the coming months: why the iron? Why not any of their books? Why not her prized first edition of *The Count of Monte Cristo*? Or her daughter's passport? Or the picture of her brother? These things and so much more were lost. But even the strongest people forfeit reason in moments of stress and panic; there is no rational explanation.

The flood had become a real threat in a matter of minutes: as Cathy reached the main floor, she heard the sound of helicopters. Ritch was busy outside, piling sacks of dirt in a last-hope defence against the water. Cathy went to the bedroom to pack a suitcase. The phone rang: it was her sister Frankie, calling to say Bowness was under an evacuation order.

I know that now! said Cathy, abruptly hanging up on her sister and continuing to pack. Once she'd filled her suitcase, she took it along with some photo albums and a few other belongings and loaded everything into the minivan; Katie and Ritch would take the car. Outside, Cathy saw police officers down the street in both directions, moving from door to door, slowly approaching their house from both sides.

She went and told Ritch and Katie about the police, and said she was leaving with Maggie. Cathy took the dog and went outside to the van. The police were now at the house next door. Is there anyone else in the house? Yes, my husband and daughter, she replied. Okay, just drive slowly through the water. We'll come talk to them in a minute.

Cathy got into the van and drove through the two and a half feet of water that had appeared on Bow Crescent, heading for her sister's house. The police soon came to the door and told Ritch the obvious: You have to leave, there's a flood.

Ritch and Katie grabbed one bag each and hurried to the car. They drove slowly, the car barely high enough to pass. It was six o'clock in the evening. As they drove away, the water was still rising, beginning to close in on their house.

KEN KNEW HE COULDN'T STAY at his friend Stu's place long. It was a small one-bedroom house, and it would soon be under an evacuation order itself the way things were going in High River. News reports were getting worse all the time, both in the town and elsewhere. Some time after his mother left with Alanna, he decided he too had better head for the city.

Driving north on Highway 2, he found plenty of traffic going the same direction, but none on the opposite side. The southbound highway was already closed. He headed for Macleod Trail and stopped at a budget hotel to find a room. To his surprise, the lobby was full of flood evacuees, a great deal of them from High River. Don't worry, the reception clerk told him, we've already got a special price worked out for flood victims.

Once he had a room, around half past six that evening, he headed out to the supermarket to buy some replacement toiletries and other things. While getting a cart, a woman commented to him about how bad the flooding was. Actually, Ken replied, I'm from High River. The woman gasped. Oh no! What's it like down there?

Ken was telling her some of the stories from his day when the woman's husband joined them. She said to Ken: Tell him what you told me. Ken briefly told the tales once more. They were amazed. We'd like to pay for your groceries.

Ken was taken aback; people don't ordinarily offer such a thing in a supermarket, particularly in the city. Well, I appreciate that, but right now money is actually the one area I'm okay in. But thank you for the gesture.

They parted warmly, and Ken went inside to find a new toothbrush.

JEREMY BROUGHT HIS RECORD COLLECTION and guitars out of the basement, and Hanna brought a few of her favourite toys up and set them on the kitchen table. Ryan came downstairs with Jeremy and offered to help pull up as many things as possible. Jeremy looked around his basement, and then looked at his friend: Ryan had spent hours carrying things up from his parents' basement, and he looked exhausted.

Jeremy shook his head. It's not worth it, he said. I'm not going to bother because it's not going to come here. We'll be fine.

Around seven o'clock that evening, Lani and Jenifer were outside barbecuing when they saw people across the street going door to door. There was a group nearby on their side of the street, and one of them called over to ask if they were telling residents to leave.

One of the doorknockers—apparently from a private security company, presumably contracted by the town—

crossed the street and spoke to the group loud enough that Lani and Jenifer could overhear: The area is being evacuated; you have to be gone by midnight; we recommend you head south to the evacuation centre in Nanton.

The women went inside the house and delivered the news. Jenifer and Ryan began gathering their things and soon left, evacuated yet again; they would head into Calgary to stay with family. Jeremy and Lani tried to think of last-minute details to take care of before leaving.

Less than thirty minutes had passed by the time the doorknockers reached their house. But now the information had changed: The highway to Nanton has been closed, and you now have to be out of your house by dusk. Lani asked if they'd be able to get to Calgary; Internet and phone service had gone out hours ago, and all they'd had for updates was the radio. The highway to Calgary is still open, they were told, but you should leave soon.

They grabbed their suitcases and loaded them into the minivan, along with the girls and the dog. They brought blankets in case they were forced to sleep in the van on the highway. The dirty dishes from supper were left on the table and countertops to be dealt with when they returned.

Just before they left, Jeremy took one last look at his 1976 Honda Civic. It was his pride and joy: he'd had a much-beloved '77 model in his youth, and he'd found this one last autumn after eleven years of searching. It was a beautiful car, with a flat black paint job, and original rims and upholstery.

I'll be back to get you tomorrow.

Jeremy got into the van and the family drove away. Their destination was south Calgary, specifically the suburban neighbourhood of McKenzie Towne where Lani's cousin lived. The area was easily accessible off the Deerfoot expressway, and high enough above the river valley to be safe from the flood. They couldn't call ahead until they regained cell phone service near Okotoks, twenty minutes south of the city.

They arrived safely, but decided to continue on to Lani's mother's house in Abbeydale, on the eastern edge of Calgary. They checked the road closures online and headed out again. It was nine o'clock when the family arrived. Once the girls were put to bed—it was well past their bedtime—Jeremy and Lani turned their full attention to the reports and rumours online, fascinated like everyone else, still feeling like they didn't have much skin in the game.

AROUND NINE O'CLOCK THURSDAY NIGHT, Steve parked his car in the Downtown West End near the Peace Bridge. He was meeting his friend Kelly for a walk along the river, but he had a lot on his mind. The women's parkour event he'd helped to organize, Varkour Day, had taken weeks of planning. Dozens of participants and instructors from Canada and the US would be arriving in Calgary the following day for the event on Saturday, which was hosted by the parkour gym he co-owned. The flood predictions had become darker, more worrying, and his concern for family and friends was growing. But all this was forgotten briefly as he reached back into his car for his crutches and felt a twinge of pain in his knee, a reminder of his recent surgery.

Steve walked slowly towards the Peace Bridge and found Kelly waiting. Kelly, a photographer, had his camera with him and was taking pictures around the bridge, the red avant-garde architecture of which tends to attract visual artists of all sorts.

Police were keeping would-be spectators back from the river, and it was clear even from a distance that the water was dangerously high and fast. Kelly and Steve wandered the area for a while before deciding to try somewhere else. They walked back to Steve's car and drove to Chinatown, where Steve pointed out a building he was considering for a new parkour gym.

The rainstorm of a few hours ago had slowed to a light shower and Kelly shared his umbrella with Steve as they walked. The two men made their way to the Centre Street Bridge, past more police and flood spectators. As they walked east, they reached the fork in the pathway just before the bridge. One option continued straight ahead and joined with the sidewalk of the upper level of the bridge; the other dipped down towards the river, running below the lower traffic deck to the other side. On a normal day, the grade of the pathway would be roughly one metre above river level at its lowest point. But the pavement had completely disappeared under grey water that reached up within nearly to the lower bridge deck, which was already closed. A police SUV was parked with lights flashing to block the pathway, as though it might otherwise appear passable.

The sun began a slow descent behind the clouds as Kelly and Steve continued on and walked up the western sidewalk of the Centre Street Bridge. The sky was dark grey, and the wind over the river was more powerful and humid than on the ground. They stood on one of the observation points jutting out from the bridge and looked west. The Bow River was so high, wide and fast as to be unrecognizable. The current crashed into the pillars of the bridge, and the violent white water contrasted with the brown-grey silt kicked up by the river.

Both men knew the river well: Steve was born in Calgary and had lived most of his twenty-eight years in the city; Kelly was an ex-Hutterite who had grown up on a colony in Manitoba, but had spent enough time as a photographer in the city to learn its nuances. Seeing such an angry, fierce version of the river they knew was startling and troubling.

Steve gingerly put weight on his knee as they walked back down the bridge to the car. The injury was an old one, dating back to 2008, but had been re-aggravated several times through his passion for aggressive skiing. His most recent surgery—a repair of his left meniscus—was only seven days old, but Steve was not one to let bodily injury or physical pain stop him from doing what he wanted, from having twenty fingers and toes in twenty different pies. He always had several projects on the go; but right then his focus was split between Varkour Day, the spectacle of the flood, and the pain radiating from his left knee.

Kelly and Steve drove farther east, parking at the Islamic centre near a popular bar and walking to the Langevin Bridge. The daylight was dimming, but darkness was still a ways off.

A steady stream of traffic moved in two lanes across the bridge into downtown as the river flowed less than a metre beneath the deck, racing past at an alarming speed. Here too the pathway was submerged and blockaded. Near the south end of the bridge, across from the Drop-In Centre, sat a police van with lights flashing. Kelly and Steve, like other passersby, alternately captured the scene on camera and stood gawking at it. The river had become a public spectacle, like a tiger in a cage whose power to harm is obvious but not directly threatening.

They wandered around a bit longer before going to meet friends elsewhere downtown, away from the sights and sounds of the river.

———————

BY EIGHT O'CLOCK THURSDAY EVENING, the signs of what was coming were too big for Tom to ignore. He called the chief of Siksika Nation, Fred Rabbit Carrier, who soon arrived at the emergency services department with three council members.

Tom briefed them on the situation. It didn't look good. The surge of water that had ripped through Canmore and Exshaw was now hitting Calgary. Ordinarily, the water flow from the city takes a day or two to reach the reserve, but the water levels at the nearby Carseland weir—which Tom was monitoring on the Alberta Environment website—were ominous. Bottom line: the water is coming, but it's not here yet. Let's get ready now.

He told them that, in his opinion, a state of local emergency declaration needed to be made proactively, before the emergency was upon them. The chief and councillors agreed. Once the order was signed, Tom was effectively the highest authority on the reserve. He held the confidence of the chief and, as a matter of respect, would never consider his authority to be above the chief and council. But he knew the reality: he was now responsible for Siksika Nation in the face of an impending crisis.

It was around ten o'clock that night by the time Tom used the emergency broadcast system to notify the populace of the state of emergency and an order of evacuation for large swaths of Siksika territory. But even before he went on the airwaves, Tom sent out a number of his crew to go door-knocking and order people out of their homes.

Sohkes was one of the firefighters sent out in an SUV borrowed from the Health Services department. He and another man were assigned a specific area of the reserve to cover. Houses were often grouped together in spread-out clusters, and Sohkes and Tim drove alongside each other before splitting up to notify different houses.

Sohkes soon found that, despite the warnings of the impending flood and the order for mandatory evacuation, most people weren't concerned. Some were partying, too drunk to reason with. Many were skeptical after the warnings in the summer of 2005, when only limited sections of the reserve flooded.

We were fine last time.

Yeah, they said we'd flood in '05, too.

It won't flood. I'm not leaving until I see the water.

The order to leave was mandatory, but they didn't have the time or manpower to force people out. All they could do was make a note of which houses refused to evacuate; the RCMP would come when they were finished their own door-knocking assignments, which could take hours.

One of the most vulnerable areas was Hidden Valley, a private community of cabins and a golf resort built on leased reserve land. Tom called the community president and told him they needed to leave as soon as possible. I want you out of there.

But Hidden Valley was counting on the normal eight-hour window of water flow from the west side of the reserve to their location further east. Tom had few options if they ignored his warnings. He repeated the order, and that was all he could do.

The next step was organizing an evacuation centre for

those who would have to leave their homes. Just behind the Health Services building is the Deerfoot Sportsplex, a large structure with a gymnasium and arena. Tom sent some of his staff over to begin setting up the one hundred forty-four cots they had in storage. He also placed a call to Merlin, the head of the Family Services department, and asked him to take charge of operating the centre.

Merlin got to work immediately. He called a large shopping centre in nearby Strathmore and asked them to put aside thirty cases of bottled water for him. As he drove with his son to pick them up, he began calling some of his key staff to make them aware of the unfolding situation and have them get down to the sportsplex.

By the time he arrived there himself, the cots had been set up. The water was brought in, and Merlin called his department's computer expert to come set up a system for registering the evacuees.

BY LATE THURSDAY EVENING, more than 75,000 residents of the city of Calgary found their homes under a mandatory evacuation order. As many as 100,000 would be forced out across the region by the end of the day. Red Deer, the third-largest city in the province, declared a state of local emergency at eight o'clock Thursday night, joining Calgary, Canmore, Bragg Creek, Cochrane, Okotoks, High River,

Lethbridge, Sundre, Black Diamond, Turner Valley, Crowsnest Pass, and several municipal districts and counties.

Thursday was panic and chaos for those directly affected, shock and wonder for those who were not. Major roads were being closed. Most bridges would be closed or restricted by Friday morning. News reports seemed unreal and worsening. The flood had come so much faster and so much worse than the predictions that anything now seemed possible. No one knew how bad it was going to get.

AROUND TEN O'CLOCK THAT EVENING, Gary was watching television at a friend's house in Brentwood when a news alert appeared. A number of communities had been under compulsory evacuation orders for hours, but this was the first Gary had heard of it. For the past several months, the Salvation Army in the Downtown East Village had been his home. But the news alert did not worry him. Even when he left his friend's home an hour later, Gary felt certain everything would be fine. After all, how in God's name would someone even close a shelter?

The rain had stopped and the evening was pleasant as Gary began the long walk from the northwest to the East Village. Gary walked everywhere as a rule, both for fitness and to save money.

It wasn't until he reached the area of 16th Avenue and 14th

Street Northwest that he began to notice something was amiss. From the ridge of North Hill, looking down at the steep descent to the inner city and the river, Gary saw that the streetlights along 14th Street were out, and much of Hillhurst was dark. He thought little of it, attributing it to the flood—which, surely, would have at least some effect on the city—and began walking downhill with the skyscrapers of downtown now looming to the southeast of him.

At the bottom, past the intersection with 5th and 6th Avenues, the street plunged into near-darkness. Gary tripped and stumbled slightly as he walked.

Must be the first time I've stumbled over my own feet because I can't see.

Hillhurst felt more like a small town than a central neighbourhood in a major city. There were few people or cars on the normally busy street. As Gary approached Memorial Drive—the scenic boulevard that traces the north shore of the Bow River across from downtown—he noticed red lights flashing off the concrete and asphalt. There were fire trucks parked there, but he couldn't see any firefighters working.

The roar of the river grew louder and louder as he passed over Memorial and continued on the Mewata Bridge over the river. Once over top of the water, the sound was deafening. The normally placid Bow was nearly invisible in the dark, but the mere sound of the water rushing past with incredible force was enough to frighten Gary.

Two men approached, walking on the same side of the bridge in the opposite direction as him. They appeared to be under the influence of something, talking loudly and stag-gering somewhat. As he neared them, one of the men put his arm out aggressively to stop Gary.

Which way does the Bow River flow? said the dishevelled man. Gary was caught off guard, but answered automatic-ally: West to east. The man seemed happy with this. Okay, go tell my buddy that, he didn't believe me... The man's arm was still blocking Gary from walking forward. Gary tried to decline and continue, but the man was insistent, and quite clearly drunk.

I'm just trying to get across the bridge.

Yeah, just go tell my buddy I was right...

Gary is a quiet man with a nervous energy. He is polite and well-spoken with a few physical tics. His demeanour is normally passive and reserved, though he does not like loud, crude people and he finds it difficult to interact with them patiently. The man blocking his path had compounded his growing discomfort with the evening, and Gary lashed out.

Go away! he shouted, knocking the man's arm out of the way and rushing past him. The man, bewildered, carried on with his friend, and Gary breathed deeply as he walked, trying to regain his composure. The roar of the river contin-ued, and the surge of the current could be felt in the bones of the bridge.

Walking east along the pathway of the river's south shore, the water became gradually more visible between the lights of Memorial on one side and the residential towers of the Downtown West End on the other. It was very high and very fast, and it would get much worse in the coming hours. It was already so high that the pathway under the Louise Bridge at 10th Street was entirely underwater. As Gary went to cross the road at bridge level, he saw a police car parked sideways in the centre of the span: the bridge was already closed.

———————————

DOM WAS IN HIS EAST VILLAGE apartment when the buses pulled up late Thursday night. Like everyone else, he'd heard the news reports predicting a worse flood than the one in 2005. But it seemed a concern for someone else until two Calgary Transit buses arrived at the Salvation Army across the street. Dom watched from his fifth-storey window as crowds of men were brought out of the building and loaded onto the buses. An evacuation was taking place metres away from his home. For the first time, well before any water appeared, Dom felt threatened by the flood.

He noticed two uniformed officials begin walking towards his building, and he quickly climbed into his wheelchair and headed for the elevator. Dom lived in Edwards Place, a subsidized housing complex in the Downtown East Village run by the Trinity Place Foundation. Like the other two Trinity buildings in the neighbourhood, it is a dated relic from the 1970s where seniors live in very modest apartments. But Edwards Place is unique in that it also houses a small handful of younger, physically disabled residents like Dom, who had lived there since a spinal stroke put him in a wheelchair three years earlier.

As Dom made his way to the ground floor, the resident caretaker was on the phone with the building manager. Lorrie lived in the only apartment on the main level. When Dom came to her door, she asked her boss to hold the line for a moment. They're evacuating the Salvation Army, he said. Things are getting bad. We should tell people to get ready. What's the plan?

Oh, really? said Lorrie. Well, I haven't heard anything yet. I'm on the phone with Ivette right now. Just tell everyone to stay in their apartments for now.

I'm not telling anyone anything, Dom said as he turned to leave. You can tell them if you like.

Dom had often clashed with Trinity officials and managers, including Lorrie and her predecessors; he had no patience for what he saw as paralysis or incompetence by the powers that be. If the homeless were being evacuated, then they ought to leave as well; of this he was certain.

A few minutes later, there was another knock at Lorrie's door: two bylaw officers, the uniformed men Dom had seen from his window. They told Lorrie that only the ground floor of Edwards Place was being evacuated, and that she would need to move to a higher apartment, and that they needed to know where she would be staying. Well, jeez, give me a minute to make a call, she said.

She made arrangements to stay on a friend's couch on a

higher floor in the building. We'll be back to put yellow tape across your door, the officers told her, and a notice of how to find you. They left and never returned.

Lorrie had been receiving calls from concerned residents asking if they would be evacuated. She had told them just what she'd told Dom: I don't know anything, stay where you are for now. The decision had now come, and her answer changed: We're not going anywhere.

Dom went back up to his apartment. It was dark outside, and there was little to see on the empty streets anyway, so he turned his flood curiosity to the Internet, following news sites and social media for the latest on evacuations and river levels. Exhausted, he went to bed around three o'clock in the morning, hoping for a few hours of rest before getting up for work.

THE DOOR-KNOCKERS CONTINUED COVERING their assigned territory on the Siksika First Nation reserve, the whole of which took about four hours. Once the initial sweep was completed, the RCMP began returning to the many homes of those who had refused to leave.

Meanwhile, Tom had also put a call in to Louise. As the coordinator for the crisis unit, she would be a crucial asset on the ground. When she arrived at the sportsplex, the evacuation centre was not much more than cots in a gymnasium. Together with Merlin's staff from Family Services, Louise began setting up key components for relief.

The reception table where evacuees would arrive and register was a priority. Louise took care to staff this station with polite, mature people who would serve as the first point of contact for displaced victims. A medical station was set up, and the canteen operator for the sportsplex was called in to prepare food.

Tom had done his best to get his hands on every available large vehicle, from SUVs to twelve-passenger mini-buses. By four o'clock in the morning, the water had arrived in earnest and the emergency services department was swamped with calls for rescue.

Many residents in flooded communities on the reserve left their houses but not the area. Instead, they lingered on the hills high above the river, waiting for hours to watch over their homes as the river rose to swallow them.

THE BIG CATS WERE TRANQUILIZED and moved off the island in crates. The birds and reptiles were caught—no small task—and evacuated, as were the primates. But prioritizing had to be done. Logical choices for which species could safely be left behind were the semi-aquatic hippos, and the towering giraffes and elephants. Aquariums of tilapia and piranhas would take too much time to safely transport, and they were also left.

One hundred fifty-eight animals were evacuated in eight hours, including half of the entire mammal population. The feat approaches miracle status when given consideration: uncooperative animals evading keepers; keepers stressed and pressed for time; limited housing facilities and transport; a shortage of crates; the ever-present danger of some species. Under normal circumstances, the capture and transport of some of the more difficult animal populations, such as the macaque monkeys, would have taken a week. To accomplish an evacuation of such a scale without death or incident amazed even those who accomplished it.

But not all were saved from the flood. Several of the peacocks that roam free around the facility were able to evade capture; four of them perished, as did many fish, and a pot-bellied pig would succumb to stress some time after the event.

The evacuation was greatly facilitated by the recent reopening of the newly renovated animal health centre. Had the flood occurred just three weeks earlier, finding temporary housing for the animals would have been far more difficult, if not impossible. One contingency plan that was widely reported but never effected was the transfer of the snow leopards, tigers and lions to the jail cells at the courthouse downtown; nevertheless, 'big cats in the big house' headlines spread the popular myth until later corrected.

EAST OF THE LOUISE BRIDGE, the pathway rose back up
out of the water, and Gary continued along it. There were a
few people here and there, marvelling at the power of the
river, wondering how bad the flood would be. Gary saw a
police car parked up ahead on the pathway. A powerful
spotlight hit him and a garbled voice came over a loud-
speaker. The orders barked at him were indiscernible, so
Gary instinctively put his hands up and began walking
slowly towards the cruiser.

What do you want? he asked when he was close enough
to be heard.

Just stay away from the river, was the reply.

The police had begun closing roads and pathways, the
start of a process that would eventually see the complete
evacuation of much of the inner city, including the entire
downtown. But Gary simply turned to take a different
route, down 4th Avenue, fully believing his shelter would be
unaffected.

He walked a few blocks before turning north towards Eau
Claire. The river was off-limits, but his curiosity was piqued
and he wanted to get as close as possible to see what sort of
damage there was. He saw a residential complex being evacuated, the residents being brought onto yellow school buses
to take them to safety.

These buildings are closer to the river than mine. Of

course they're going to flood. But the shelter should still be fine.

In some areas, there was a good deal of water on the street, the storm sewers having overfilled with the rising river levels and backed up through the drains. A white van drove through the intersection near the federal Harry Hayes building with water nearly up to the top of its tires. Images of flooded New Orleans flashed through Gary's mind as it struck him that this would be a far worse emergency than the 2005 flood. Still, he believed that his shelter would be untouched, that he would be unaffected so long as he could reach that safe haven.

Gary proceeded through Chinatown, past Centre Street, walking in the direction of the Langevin Bridge where he hoped to get a better view of the river. But it was nearly one o'clock now, and it occurred to him that he ought to get to the shelter before it got too late. He decided to turn south and go see the river tomorrow.

Outside the Salvation Army shelter on 9th Avenue Southeast, he encountered another resident who told him the shelter was closed. I don't know what's going on, said the man, but I'm going to bed. He laid down on a bench outside the building. Gary approached the doors of the shelter, which were tied with police caution tape. A notice was posted on one of the doors: These premises are closed by order of the Calgary Emergency Management Authority. An unfamiliar figure was inside the darkened building; Gary knocked on the glass, but the figure turned away.

It was his worst nightmare: homeless in the middle of a natural disaster that already promised to be much worse than anyone had expected. Gary went through his list of close friends in his mind, ruling out all the potential options for shelter. It was the middle of the night, and he had nowhere to go. I guess I might as well go look at the river now, he thought.

The Salvation Army is just a couple blocks west of the confluence of the Bow and Elbow Rivers at Fort Calgary. Gary headed to RiverWalk, the redeveloped pathway and public space that had opened less than a year earlier. The multimillion dollar project was already largely underwater, with LED lights shining up from below. The water was only a few hundred metres from Fort Calgary.

From his vantage point on a grassy hill, Gary could see the two rivers: the Elbow was swollen to the normal size of the Bow; the Bow was some other beast entirely, roaring and surging with frightening force. The mingling point of the waters was a white, churning whirlpool. Gary marvelled at the power of it all, and began to realize that he needed to find somewhere to go before things got worse.

He knew of a shelter on Southland Drive—well south of downtown—and he decided that was his best option. Gary had an aversion to aggressive or rowdy behaviour, and was therefore loathe to consider the Drop-In Centre, which was far closer but had a reputation in his mind for playing host to those qualities. So Gary walked west to Macleod Trail and headed south, under the Canadian Pacific rail tracks that separate downtown from the Beltline communities of Connaught and Victoria Park. He soon had on his left the Stampede grounds, which were to host the world's most famous rodeo in a couple weeks.

Just south of 18th Avenue, Gary's plan unravelled: the Pattison Bridge, which carries southbound Macleod Trail over the Elbow, was completely submerged with only the railings visible above the water.

Think, think, think: where can you go? What about cutting through Mission and trying the 25th Avenue bridge? Maybe it's higher, maybe it's still okay.

But it wasn't. The historic district of Mission was already beginning to flood. There was enough water in some areas that garbage cans and recycling bins were floating away. The expensive homes on the prime real estate along the Elbow were already under seige. Decks and verandas gave way as the water washed away the earth; one house had already partially collapsed. The area had been under an evacuation order for hours, and the 25th Avenue bridge was also flooded. On 4th Street, the quaint main street of Mission, the water had filled the street south of 25th Avenue.

With all his southbound routes seemingly closed, Gary was increasingly worried as he walked north, trying to think of any options available to him in that direction. He retraced his route back to Macleod Trail and walked towards downtown. Then he remembered St. Mary's Church, where he'd gone a few times for their free Sunday supper, and he made a left turn on 17th Avenue and walked west.

In the parking lot outside the church, he encountered a man talking on a cell phone. Gary stopped and waited to speak to him; then he noticed that the doors of St. Mary's High School were open, so he left the man and went inside to the gymnasium.

There were rows and rows of elderly people sleeping on cots, cramped close together. The sight struck Gary deeply, and the stress and anger that had been building inside him on his frustrating search dissipated. Remember, you're not the only one with problems tonight.

He went back outside to the man. Gary listened to his phone conversation: ...where are we going to get breakfast for all these people? Yeah. I don't know. Okay, call me back...

Gary waited patiently. When the man had finished, Gary briefly explained his situation. I'm sorry, we're completely full, said the man with sympathy. Well, do you know of any other places that have room? He did not.

Gary thanked him and left. He walked north through Rouleauville Square, then along 1st Street Southwest. There were two city workers erecting barricades and he approached them.

Can you tell me where I can find a place to sleep?

Oh, okay, said one of them, pulling out his phone. He dialled 3-1-1, the City's all-purpose public contact line, and waited on hold for several minutes before connecting with an operator.

Yeah, there's a guy here whose shelter got closed, and he

can't get south because he's on foot, what is he supposed to do?

The worker relayed the operator's advice to Gary: there was a shelter set up at Centre Street Church. Gary knew the church; it was up at Centre and 40th Street, at least an hour's walk uphill. It was now nearly dawn, and Gary was ready to consider the idea of sleeping somewhere outside rather than continuing his seemingly hopeless trek. He thanked the worker and kept walking.

He came to 11th Avenue and turned east. With the Calgary Tower looming over him, he approached the Mustard Seed. A staff member outside told him they were full up. You can try the DI, he said, referring to the Drop-In Centre near the river. Isn't it closed? asked Gary with some surprise. Naw, it's open. Are you sure? Yeah, I've been sending people there all night.

Gary began walking back into downtown. He was afraid of the DI, though he'd never actually stayed there. His idea of it was informed by rumours and stories, some real, some exaggerated. His imagination was filled with all the worst stereotypes of homelessness: of rowdy drunks shouting and fighting, of mental illness, of crowds and noise. But there were no other options. It was crazy to think of sleeping on the street, he knew that, and Centre Street Church was too far away. The DI was all that was left.

The Calgary Drop-In and Rehab Centre is housed in a modern flatiron building in the East Village on Riverfront Avenue—which, as the name suggests, is not a desirable address during a major flood. Gary could see some water already on the street as he approached.

Hey, that's my bag!

A man was walking towards Gary and yelling at him. You stole my bag!

It's not yours, it's mine, I didn't steal it.

Yeah, it's mine, give it back, asshole!

I don't know if he's drunk or high, Gary thought, but something's not right upstairs.

Look, said Gary, it's my bag, it has my stuff in it. Just leave me alone!

Gimme my bag back! Give it back! The man was yelling at him, and people on the street outside the DI were now watching curiously. Gary tried walking away, but the man wouldn't leave him. Hey! Gimme my bag back!

It's not your bag! Gary screamed at him. It's not your bag! It's not your bag! Exhaustion and stress had worn him down to the ground, and the man's provocations had been more than he could bear civilly. The man was taken aback, perhaps even frightened, and turned and walked away in some confusion.

Gary arrived at the DI. A few people were outside milling about. He approached a man in a staff shirt. Excuse me, do you work for the DI? Yeah, what do you want? I need to get in, I need to stay here. Nope, sorry, pal.

There was a female staff member outside as well, and Gary went over to her and asked the same question. We're being evacuated, she said.

Maybe she's just being dramatic, thought Gary. But shortly a stream of people poured out of the building and began making their way as one herd towards the Langevin Bridge.

Gary joined the crowd; it seemed as good an option as any at that point. As they neared the bridge, Gary saw police cars with lights flashing and reporters waiting with photographers and TV cameras. The evacuation of the homeless from downtown Friday morning would be one of the first stories to put a human face on the disaster. The group crossed the bridge, and gathered in the parking lot of a gas station across Memorial Drive.

Gary sat on a rock and listened to the coarser, louder men of the group make jokes and banter with one another; people like that irritated him. The downtown skyscrapers were beginning to shine in the sunrise. The people who worked in them were mostly still sleeping, still unaware that they would be told to stay home today.

FRIDAY

Southern Alberta doesn't have tornados or hurricanes. There are no earthquakes or tsunamis. There are instead two types of local disasters: hailstorms and floods, both of which can be devastating.

The Blackfoot knew not to camp near the Bow in the spring and early summer; other rivers were equally dangerous. But when the first frontier towns were established—Canmore, Cochrane, High River, Calgary—the settlers sought proximity to rivers for drinking water, power, sanitation and trade. Homes and businesses were built close to the water initially, but after the early floods, many of these were rebuilt further back, and wary homesteaders began looking for higher ground. But whether on the east shore of the Elbow in Inglewood or, later, on the west shore in the East Village and downtown, Calgary was always close to the edge of disaster.

One of the largest floods, though unmeasured, occurred in 1897, when the river rose an estimated five metres and swamped the small city, washing out the railway line to the coast. Similarly severe disasters struck in 1879 and 1902; these three floods still stand as the largest to have ever hit the city, larger even than 2013. But there were comparatively few permanent structures at that time, and the level of destruction was nowhere near what it would be when modern Calgary was inundated.

In 1915, the Centre Street Bridge, also known as the MacArthur Bridge, was washed away; the present structure would replace it the following year. Severe floods in Calgary, Okotoks, High River and elsewhere would occur again in 1923 and 1929. In June 1932, the city received nearly the entire monthly rainfall average in twenty-four hours. The resulting flood would have been far more damaging if not for the capacious recently-built Glenmore Reservoir, which took in enough water to fill it from nearly empty to within inches of cresting after two days. Had the flood been a year earlier, the dam would not yet have been completed to stop the water; had it been a year later, the reservoir would have been full and quickly spilled over.

High River was also notorious for its seasonal floods. The 1932 event hit hard and stood as the record for decades. Other serious floods occurred in 1923, 1929, 1952, 1953, and 1963. Then, in 1995, a record-breaking disaster struck the town and other areas, causing $100 million in damages.

In 2005, rain storms soaked southern Alberta and a massive flood resulted, with unprecedented evacuations in Calgary. Other communities, such as Okotoks, Red Deer and especially High River, were also hard hit. The total cost was estimated at $400 million. Many homes and businesses were lost. Forty municipalities suffered damages; fourteen declared states of local emergency. Four lives were lost.

But the 2005 flood saw the Bow River peak at 791 cubic-metres per second (m^3/s), roughly half of the peak flow of the 1932 flood. The damage was so extensive because the city had grown large, with expensive homes and infrastructure, and denser populations than in the first half of the 20th century.

Though now largely forgotten in the public mind, one of the most significant disasters in Calgary's history was not a flood, but the great fire of 1886. On November 7 of that year, in the early morning hours, flames appeared at the rear wall of Parish & Son's grocery store, near where the Calgary Tower stands today. The fire spread quickly in the settlement of largely wooden buildings, and the church bells were rung loudly to awaken the residents.

The fire department—established the previous year as the Calgary Hook, Ladder and Bucket Corps—fought the flames for hours with water and a recently-ordered chemical engine. Untouched buildings were torn down in a desperate attempt to stop the blaze. In all, fourteen buildings were lost and damages were estimated above $100,000 (more than $2 million today).

The destruction was a significant blow to the small Prairie community, but the lasting legacy of the fire was a law drafted by city officials stating that all large downtown buildings were now required to be built from Paskapoo sandstone. Deposits of the stone were easy to come by in the region, and as many as fifteen quarries soon opened around Calgary in a mining boom that would last until the start of the First

World War. In less than fifteen years, some forty sandstone structures were erected, many of them enduring landmarks, and Calgary became known as the Sandstone City.

One such building was the old City Hall, later designated a national historic site, and still home to the offices of the mayor and city aldermen when it filled with floodwater on Friday morning.

Calgary awoke to worsening circumstances. The downtown had been closed, and trains and buses were not running into the city centre. The City had requested people stay home from work. Both the public and Catholic boards closed their schools for the day. Around half past seven, the City-owned electric utility began shutting off power to flooded areas, including the downtown. Because of the nature of the power grid, these outages could not be precise, and many unaffected and unevacuated areas were left without electricity as well.

Meanwhile, the media hub of Toronto, two hours ahead of Alberta, was churning out headlines and stories for the national newspapers and wire services. International media had picked up on the story overnight, leading with the most dramatic images, such as High River's disappeared streets, or the skyscrapers of Calgary looking like a modern Venice arranged on a watery grid.

DOM WOKE EARLY FRIDAY MORNING after only a few hours of sleep. He was due to be at his job by nine o'clock and he needed to allow plenty of time for travelling to work. Simple things like taking the train can often be needlessly complicated for wheelchair users.

He got into his chair and went to the window: both 9th Avenue and 3rd Street were filled with water in front of Edwards Place, as was the 4th Street underpass. Dom grabbed his laptop and furiously scanned news sites and social media, getting caught up on the situation. The rivers had risen dramatically overnight and the inner city, among other areas, was paralyzed. There was no transit service downtown, and now Dom had no way to get to work.

He called his boss and told him he'd have to stay home. No, we really need you, said Ralph. It's inventory day. I'll come downtown and pick you up.

GARY WAS NOT FROM CALGARY. He'd grown up in northern Alberta and moved to the big city of the south at the age of twenty-six. That was eighteen years ago, and Calgary was then a very different place in many ways. Gary immediately fell in love with the city. He'd been to Edmonton, Vancouver, Toronto, Montreal, but in Calgary something clicked. It felt like home.

He started a travel tourism program at the Southern

Alberta Institute of Technology, but he quit six months later when he became fearful that the coming Internet age would make travel agents obsolete. Eight years of call centre work followed, and then various odd jobs. He began developing sleeping problems, unable to sleep, sleeping for fifteen hours at a time, showing up tired or late for work. Jobs became more difficult to hold.

When the family farm up north was sold, Gary's share of the money was quite substantial. A sudden influx of serious money inspires various reactions in different people: some see an opportunity to invest in a dream; some spend it quickly on vacations or big-ticket items; Gary decided to live frugally on the windfall for as long as he possibly could, and he soon stopped working entirely.

The money lasted ten years. By then, Gary's sleep disorder had grown more disruptive, and his resume held a suspicious seven-year gap. He had little experience or train-ing. With no money and no prospects, facing bills and rent he couldn't pay, he became desperate. He decided to kill himself by jumping off the balcony of his eleventh-floor apartment. But when he tried, he felt unable to, sensing a hand pushing him back. He gave up and called 9-1-1, and was taken to hospital.

That was July 4, 2012. By the time of the flood one year later, Gary would be on financial aid, living at the Salvation Army, trying to find a way to get his life back together. Calgary had become synonymous with money and oppor-tunity, but not for everyone: on any given night, 3,500 people are homeless, and one hundred sixty families sleep in shelters; 14,000 households are considered at risk of homelessness.

Early Friday morning, after waiting impatiently for some time, Gary approached a DI staff member and asked what was happening to the evacuees who had been gathered across the river from downtown. He was told that the clients—the DI's preferred term for the people who use the shelter—were to be taken by bus to a new location where a temporary shelter would be set up. Gary explained his situation and asked if he could come; of course he could.

Several city buses soon pulled up to the cheers of the homeless, and they piled onto them. Gary found himself squeezed to the back of one bus; there would be forty needed in all. As it filled up, the smells began to overwhelm Gary.

Don't fart in my face! someone yelled. Another shouted: Drive this fucking bus to Tijuana!

The quieter passengers spoke amongst themselves, but Gary said nothing to anyone as the buses drove in a convoy up Edmonton Trail to McKnight Boulevard, far away from the rivers. We're fucking here! someone yelled as the buses stopped and everyone got off. They were at a former hotel in the northeast of the city, which had been purchased by the Drop-In Centre a few years ago with the intention of turning it into affordable housing. But it still sat unused and empty, and with a sudden evacuation order and nowhere to go, the DI staff had rushed to get in touch with the City for the permits and approval needed for temporary occupancy.

I get a room to myself!

Hey, don't touch me, man!

Nice fucking digs, eh!

The crowd was taken inside and downstairs to a large conference room. The building had no food, no supplies. The kitchen was unusable without inspections and permits for the exhaust system. The first evacuees had arrived around half past seven that morning, and within a short period of time the donations began coming in: food, water bottles, clothing, blankets, toiletries. The building was known in the residential community that surrounded it as there was on-going debate and some opposition regarding the Drop-In Centre's future use of it.

But the support that poured in was remarkable, with some residents bringing in crockpots full of homecooked food later in the day. Restaurants and businesses would send seemingly unlimited supplies of pizzas, coffee, and doughnuts, and several food trucks arrived to hand out free fast food.

Inside, the DI staff were trying to strategize and organize, attempting to adapt procedures and best-practices from the regular shelter to this unequipped building.

Gary was near exhaustion. His all-night quest had left him drained. All he wanted was sleep, but he could do nothing but wait for a bed.

Sandwiches and pizza were served around noon. Gary wasn't hungry, but he ate anyway. Midway through the meal, he hit a wall. He felt he might fall asleep on his plate.

He went to several staff members and asked if he could

have somewhere to rest. No, the sleeping arrangements aren't set up yet, he was told. Finally, he asked someone who said yes: she took him to the former billiards room and lounge of the hotel, where a makeshift medical clinic had been set up. She managed to find him a sleeping bag and a blanket. Do you need anything else? she asked kindly. Just sleep, said Gary, thank you so much.

She left, and he made a bed beside empty milk crates and tanks of carbon dioxide from the former bar and laid down. He immediately fell into a deep sleep and didn't wake up until the next day.

———————

DOM DRESSED FOR WORK and headed downstairs. Once at ground level, he saw just how deep the water on the street was, and it made him nervous. His boss Ralph had picked up another employee downtown and they arrived in a van, which was high enough to make it through the water when approaching from the west.

I don't think I should go, Dom protested. I have a bad feeling about this, I think it's going to get worse.

Look, said Ralph, come with us now and I'll drive you back home if things get worse. Okay?

Dom agreed and got in, and they drove slowly through the water on 9th Avenue. Not long after they left, the power went out in the building.

Sam lived on the fourth floor of Edwards Place, one floor below her friend Dom. At twenty-seven, she was one of the youngest residents in the building, fourteen years younger than Dom. Sam had been born with spinal bifida, a condition that required her to use a wheelchair to get around.

She woke up around a quarter to nine when she heard muffled voices in the hallway. It was an announcement on the building's public address system, though it was difficult to understand everything: We're here in the building... you've been flooded... plan to get you out...

Sam was tired; like Dom, she'd stayed up late trying to follow the flood online. She got out of bed and into her wheelchair and went to her west-facing window. She looked down into the adjoining courtyard that Edwards Place shared with the Municipal Building, the shining glass structure many times the size of the old City Hall that housed the city government. The small courtyard was flooded, but it was difficult to tell how much water was down there. Sam went to the bathroom, but the light wouldn't turn on. She went into the hallway to look out the window by the elevator, which had an east view. The streets had vanished under muddy rivers dotted with trees. There was no activity, not a person or moving car in sight. Sam took a picture of the scene with her phone and posted it online.

If the fire department is here, she reasoned, I guess there's nothing to do but wait.

The resident caretaker of Edwards Place had left early that morning, well before any signs of trouble. After going back into her apartment to shower, Lorrie had left at half past five and driven to her second job in the northeast quadrant of the city. There had been no water on the street, no problem with the building at all. But around nine o'clock, she began receiving calls from residents about the power being about, about the streets flooding, about whether or not they'd be evacuated. Lorrie told her boss she had to go home.

IN 1875, FATHER CONSTANTINE SCOLLEN established his third Catholic mission in the Calgary area. The first had been forty kilometres west of the fort, the second was near the confluence. The third was a permanent settlement on the twisting Elbow River upstream of Fort Calgary. This was the beginning of what would eventually become the historic Mission district of Calgary.

Eight years later, Father Albert Lacombe, a missionary from Lower Canada who had spent more than thirty years in the West, began the acquisition of land around the mission. He wanted to build a strong community, a haven for francophone Catholics in southern Alberta. In 1899, the village of Rouleauville was incorporated, named for Charles Rouleau and his brother Edouard, prominent members of the local francophone community who had promoted the idea of a French-speaking village in the area.

The street names were French-Canadian, prefaced with 'rue'. Landmarks included the Couvent du Sacré-Coeur, L'église Sainte-Mary, and the mission itself, Notre-Dame de la Paix. A road, today known as Mission Road, wound its way down to the community from Macleod Trail, and in 1886, the first Mission Bridge was built across the river.

But the French-Canadian culture of the area was soon sapped away by the larger anglophone city. In 1907, Rouleauville was annexed to become part of Calgary, and renamed Mission. The French names of the streets were changed to fit with the city's newly adopted numbered grid; the northern boundary road of Rouleauville, rue Notre-Dame, became 17th Avenue South.

The neighbourhood's main commercial district, 4th Street, continued to be important in the life of the city, gaining streetcar service in 1909. From the late 20th century, with an influx of wealth in Calgary, the area evolved into a trendy arts district, with many small, popular local businesses.

The area, though, was topographically low in relation to the nearby river. On Friday morning, the neighbourhood's southern portion was largely submerged. The floodwaters stretched for several blocks along 4th Street and other roads. Nearby neighbourhoods such as Roxboro, Erlton, Elbow Park, Parkhill, and Elboya were also swamped.

So too were Sunnyside, Hillhurst, and Bridgeland on the north shore of the Bow across from downtown. The low, flat riverfront neighbourhood of Chinatown was heavily inundated. Upstream along the Bow, Bowness and Montgomery were hit, while Discovery Ridge and Tsuu T'ina First Nation felt the force of the Elbow upstream of the Glenmore Reservoir. Tens of thousands of residents had been evacuated from more than two dozen city neighbourhoods overnight, many of them leaving ahead of the rising waters. It wasn't until the daylight of Friday morning that the news cameras were able to capture the incredible shots of the water, metres deep in many areas.

Photographs of the devastation in High River and Canmore, among others, were shocking and hard-hitting. But this was the first time a major Canadian city had been so extensively flooded, so clearly on its knees before the rising waters. The images of the most identifiably Calgarian landmarks—the Calgary Tower, the Saddledome and Stampede grounds, the twisted tracks of the C-Train, the downtown skyscrapers and City Hall—as well as the aerial shots of the city stunned everyone who saw them.

On Friday morning, a local sports writer began posting photos online of water surrounding the Saddledome, the city's major arena and home to the NHL's Calgary Flames. A photo would emerge Saturday showing the water up to the tenth row of seats. The dressing rooms, electronic equipment, integral infrastructure and a great number of irreplaceable history items were under metres of floodwater. The thought of so much water inside the arena made anything seem possible.

PARKOUR ISN'T EXACTLY A SPORT. It's better described as a non-competitive training discipline. In essence, the goal is to move as quickly and efficiently as possible through an environment, overcoming obstacles with grace and agility while maintaining momentum. Running, jumping, climbing, rolling, swinging are all combined fluidly; a person may only use their body and physical environment to move forward.

Since originating in France in the 1980s, parkour has spread worldwide as an athletic endeavour requiring nothing more than a person and a suitable environment, usually urban. It lends itself to the age of viral video with its simple yet remarkable feats of movement and graceful speed.

Varkour Day was to be an event aimed at getting women interested in the activity. There would be an instructional workshop, outdoor parkour jam sessions, and an after-party in the evening. People were planning to come in from places like Edmonton, Grande Prairie, Seattle and Colorado for the event. All of this, however, was under threat Friday morning.

Steve was stunned by how much things had worsened overnight. Most of the bridges in and out of downtown were closed; there were evacuation orders in more than two dozen neighbourhoods in the city.

He discussed the options with Matt and Frankie—his co-owners of the parkour gym—and Andrea, who had originated the idea of Varkour Day. People would be coming to

Calgary later that day, and a decision needed to be made about whether the event was still feasible.

The gym was in the south of the city, fully accessible and away from the danger. But Olympic Plaza and Eau Claire, key locations for other portions of the event, were in the evacuation zone downtown.

The Eau Claire neighbourhood derives its name from one of the earliest major businesses in Calgary, the Eau Claire and Bow River Lumber Company. The name, French for 'clear water', came not from Quebec but rather Eau Claire, Wisconsin, from where the sawmill was relocated. By digging a channel to allow easier transport of logs floating from Kananaskis to the sawmill, the company inadvertantly created a large island in the Bow River, which was named for the sawmill's founder Peter Anthony Prince.

Now a beautiful and popular park, Prince's Island had been a backup venue for Varkour Day; but the island was submerged under several metres of water.

To make things more complicated, Calgary Transit had shut down a number of bus routes, as well as train service in the downtown core, which meant that transportation would be a major issue.

These were the things they didn't have. But what they did have was Century Gardens, a public park downtown at 8th Avenue and 8th Street Southwest. The park was popular in the parkour community for its rather unusual concrete Brutalist structures which, while obscuring sightlines and giving the area a somewhat dated feel, served as a perfect obstacle course for parkour. Though it was downtown, Century Gardens sat just outside the evacuation zone.

The after-party Saturday evening was to be held at a bar in the Beltline district of Connaught, just across the Canadian Pacific tracks that delineate downtown proper; this part of the itinerary was also still feasible.

The decision was made by the group to proceed with a modified Varkour Day. The event might not be what was originally envisioned, but it could still serve its function as a catalyst for women to try parkour. After all, Steve told the others, that's precisely what parkour is: adapting to your surroundings as best you can while moving forward.

———————————————

AFTER FLEEING THEIR HOME on Bow Crescent, Ritch and Cathy went to stay with her sister Frankie. Ritch soon opted to sleep on a couch at the Shrine Centre in Bowness where he worked, as it lessened the crowd in the house and saved him from commuting. Their son went to stay with his girlfriend. Katie stayed with her boyfriend. Cathy continued going to her job at a telecommunications company, since the office was safely in the northeast. Staying busy helped distract them from the thoughts and worries about the house, but it was never out of mind for long.

On Friday and Saturday, Cathy met with a neighbour of theirs on the Varsity cliffs along Bowmont Park, overlooking

Bowness across the river. The vantage point was crowded with spectators and gawkers. Looking down at Bow Crescent, Cathy could see the entire street was a muddy river. It was hard to tell where the Bow ended and Bowness began. She knew that the damage would be bad.

WHEN LOUISE RETURNED TO THE Deerfoot Sportsplex at eight o'clock Friday morning, the Siksika evacuation centre was beginning to fill. The handful of staff were doing their best to attend to the needs of the evacuees, who were turning up at a rate of about fifteen per hour. With the state of emergency declared, Tom was de facto in charge of the entire reserve, and Merlin was tasked with overseeing the evacuation centre; but they both had a great many matters to attend to, and the ground-level operation of the relief effort fell to Louise and Adrienne, whom Merlin had delegated from Family Services.

Both women had taken the same emergency management training, and they followed the handbook's advice on setting up a relief centre. The largest problem was the lack of manpower. Though volunteers from unaffected areas of the reserve had begun turning up with offers to help, the influx of evacuees outstripped them. Louise and Adrienne scrambled to set up stations, instruct staff and distribute needed items.

In her day job in the crisis unit, Louise regularly dealt with the human impact of suicides, grief and sudden deaths. She was used to seeing people at their most devastated and raw. But as evacuees arrived at the sportsplex, the depair on their faces began to wear her down, each one leaving a small mark on her, gradually accumulating into something more. Many were sombre. Others were crying.

One couple arrived soaking wet. They'd become cut off by the water and had to be rescued from their home. They held each other as though it was all they had left.

Some people were distraught over leaving their spiritual bundles behind in their homes during the rush to flee. The bundles are a significant part of Blackfoot spirituality, and are treated as living beings. To be a bundle holder is a great and sacred responsibility, and the thought of the precious items being swept away by the river was too much for some to bear.

Already known in the community for her role as a crisis worker, Louise was sought out by distraught residents in search of consolation. They would approach her with tearful eyes and shaky voices and need her to be stronger than they were. But the chaos of the relief centre continued unabated, and Louise performed nonstop juggling acts of staff needs and victim counselling.

JEREMY AND LANI GOT PRECIOUS little sleep that first night away from their home. Between news reports, social media, and phone conversations with friends, they heard details and stories of varying accuracy: there were blockades to stop residents from returning to High River; the army was being called in; many people were refusing to leave; many people were dead. It was difficult to separate truth from rumour, and they didn't know what to believe on a day when everything they took for granted had been turned upside-down. There was no official word on the severity of the flooding, and the media had no access to evacuated areas.

They sat next to each other with their computers for much of Friday. It was a full house: Lani's sister and mother lived together. Her sister left for work during the day, but her mother worked from home. Between the two young girls, the dog, and Jeremy and Lani's growing stress and distraction, things were hectic at best, tense at worst. Fortunately, Lani's mother took charge of wrangling the kids while their parents tried to piece together from afar what was happening in High River.

They assumed that their house had indeed been flooded; it sounded as though few areas of the town had escaped unscathed. But until someone could tell them about their specific neighbourhood on the east side of town, it was all a guessing game.

A High River flood support page on Facebook had appeared, and this proved to be a source for both information and rumour, first-hand accounts mixed in with speculation and exaggeration. In a vacuum, people will breathe any air that comes to them.

A friend shared a news video with Lani's on social media Friday afternoon. It was footage of the town from a police motorboat that cruised along the flooded streets. Suddenly, one minute and fifty-five seconds into the video, their house appeared. There was about five feet of water outside their house, reaching as high as the front porch. Five feet, as high as the porch.

It was shattering. Lani broke down upon watching it. They had prepared themselves for some damage, some water in the basement. But they were not at all ready for that sight: five feet of water, as high as the porch. That meant the basement was completely submerged; the water was almost certainly on the main floor of the house. It was as though the bottom had suddenly fallen out of their world. Jeremy consoled his wife as she cried. He tried to be strong for her in that moment, but the truth was that they were both completely gutted.

LORRIE DROVE SOUTH ON EDMONTON TRAIL as far as Memorial Drive. There she found police cars blocking the Langevin Bridge into downtown. The police told her she would not be allowed to cross the river.

But there's a building of seniors and disabled people, and

they need me, I'm the caretaker, and there's no one else there, I have to get there.

Well, you can't cross the bridge. It's not safe.

There must be some other way, I have to get there, they have no one else and their power is out.

Well, if you want, you can walk across the 5th Avenue bridge. But I can't let you drive.

Lorrie parked her van at a nearby gas station and headed out on foot. There are four bridges in the immediate area: the Langevin Bridge, lowest and oldest, connects southbound 4 Street across the river; the 5th Avenue bridge, connecting traffic exiting downtown to both northbound Edmonton Trail and eastbound Memorial Drive; the LRT bridge, which carries trains between the median of Memorial and downtown; and the 4th Avenue flyover, which soars high above the others as it brings traffic from westbound Memorial to 4th Avenue downtown.

Lorrie crossed the bridge to 5th Avenue, which was devoid of traffic. The bridge curves as it enters downtown, landing at the intersection of 5th Avenue and 3rd Street Southeast. Here Lorrie saw for the first time what had happened in the span of only a few hours: the street was entirely under water several feet deep, with a fire truck blocking the route south. She approached the firefighters who were sitting on the truck.

I have to get through, I have to get to my building, she said, explaining the situation. The firefighters tried to talk her out of it: It's dangerous, it's deep, we don't know what condition the pavement is in under the water. I need to go, she insisted. Maybe you could drive me in your truck?

No, we can't do that.

Lorrie smiled. Maybe one of you wouldn't mind giving me a piggy-back ride? The men laughed at this. No, sorry.

Well, look, said one of them, if you really want to go and walk through, I'll come escort you to make sure you get there safely.

Lorrie agreed. Together they began walking into the water. The water was quite cold and dirty, and she was soon submerged in it up to her waist. Her escort stayed beside her, ready to grab her should she fall. With so much water on the road, there was a possibility the asphalt could crack if the ground beneath it was washed away.

It was four blocks to Edwards Place, and Lorrie felt her muscles struggling from the cold after two. It was slow going, both for cautious footing and the resistence of the water, but they reached their destination and went inside. It was dark in the building, and the firefighter turned on his flashlight so Lorrie could see well enough to open her apartment and find a change of clothes.

———————————

SEAN WAS IN SOUTHERN ONTARIO to see his newborn niece when the phone calls and emails started. The images of the flood had by then spread across the country and around the world. Sean knew his condo in Varsity high above Bowmont Park was safe, but he was still concerned for his adopted city, and for what his role in the disaster would be.

The phone calls and emails were the first step. As a lieutenant in the Calgary Highlanders army reserve infantry regiment, he commanded a platoon of thirty-five men. The chain of command is fundamental in the Canadian Forces, and it is standard practice to test the lines of communication in advance of an impending mission. Seeing the scale of the devastation in Alberta, Sean was not surprised to get word from his superiors: Be prepared to task.

The Highlanders had stood down for the summer as usual, but they were required to maintain their ability to deploy domestically on short notice should the need arise. The communications fan-out was practised four times a year: commanding officers contact the level below them in the chain of command, who in turn contact the personnel under them. Each level is asked to report back their status and availability to deploy so that a picture of how many people are available can be developed and a plan to deploy can be formulated if necessary. Sean emailed everyone in his platoon and had thirty-five responses back within a day. They were ready.

Sean packed his bag. The flood indeed looked like a significant disaster for which they could be deployed; but even had it been doubtful that the phone call would come, he would have been packed and prepared regardless. When the order came, he headed straight for Pearson Airport in Toronto to catch the next flight to Calgary.

I'm sorry, sir, the airline representative told him, but I'll have to charge you a penalty for bumping your flight up.

Well, you know, I'm a soldier and I just got called to Calgary to help with the floods.

I'm sorry, sir, it's just our policy.

Sean touched down at Calgary International early Friday evening. His girlfriend was waiting for him, and she drove him to his condo in Varsity to collect his military gear. He packed and prepared what he would need, then took a walk to the edge of the cliffs in Bowmont Park.

The Bow River was swollen and angry, the unusual roar of it quite audible from up high. Large parts of Bowness were submerged. The reality of it hit home for Sean in a way that news reports can't effect. This is really happening. Then, with an instinct bred from training, he shifted from citizen to soldier. Game face on, we're going.

LAWRENCE RETURNED TO EDWARDS PLACE around the same time as Lorrie. He had first come on foot around six o'clock that morning to assess any immediate threats to the Trinity buildings. He saw the water on the streets, away from the building, and then moved down 9th Avenue to examine Murdoch Manor and King Tower. The flooded 4th

Street underpass struck him as incredible but not threatening, and the CEO of the Trinity Place Foundation was optimistic that they could ride out the disaster without an evacuation.

Edwards Place had been running on an emergency generator for a few hours, which provided power to one elevator, stairwell lighting, and a few other essentials—but no electricity in the suites. An order from the fire department had come down instructing them to shelter in place; this meant provisions needed to be made for feeding the residents while the kitchen was without power. No one would or could say for certain how long they would have to stay there.

A maintainance worker from Trinity went in his truck to buy food and supplies, driving westward on 9th Avenue, where the water was relatively low and passable. Using the barbecue on the second storey balcony, Trinity workers and executives spent the day cooking hamburgers and hotdogs for residents. Some were distraught or frustrated, some were optimistic and determined. Food and drinks were brought up to those most vulnerable residents who were unable to come down to the balcony.

At some point during Friday afternoon, the backup generators at Edwards Place gave out. Now there was no elevator access in the seventeen storey building, no light at all in the stairwells. The emergency sump pump that had been working to mitigate the amount of water in and around the building stopped. Staff, caretakers and personal care aides continued their work reassuring residents, making and delivering barbecued food, and carrying fresh oxygen tanks up many flights of stairs. Residents who had come down to the common balcony on the second floor were escorted back up the dark stairwells to their suites.

Trinity's director of operations called 9-1-1 and explained that shelter-in-place was no longer a reasonable option for such a vulnerable population. The situation was acknowledged on the other end of the phone, but no firm timeline was given for an evacuation of the buildings.

Meanwhile, on the fourth floor of Edwards Place, Sam had tried to keep tabs on the situation online. Her phone and computer were not fully charged, and their batteries drained to nothing in a couple hours. She spent much of the day next to the window by the elevator, where she had a better view. From there she could sometimes see a few of the people on the balcony below, but without power to the elevators, she had no way to go down there.

Some of the care workers had come knocking on doors to see if residents wanted burgers or coffee. One of them gave Sam a flashlight. Aside from those few visits, she was mostly alone, watching through the window. The streets were completely deserted, and she wondered why they hadn't been evacuated yet; no one seemed to know what was happening. As the hours ticked by, Sam began to feel trapped and abandoned. Her frustration began giving way to fear.

THE VARKOUR DAY ORGANIZERS POSTED the changes to the event online, with an additional caution to only attend if it was safe and reasonable to do so. Participants travelling from elsewhere in the province began arriving later that day. Meanwhile, Steve and a few others went to Scotsman's Hill, a popular vantage point overlooking the Stampede grounds and parts of the inner city.

The landscape was devastated: the Stampede grounds were completely submerged under metres of water; random objects floated by. The Elbow River, which runs along the east and south of the grounds, had completely swallowed parking lots, animal pens, the rodeo area, even the chuck-wagon track, which has a circumference of over a kilometre. Even the Grandstand stage—a massive wheeled contraption that gets pulled out each night during the event—appeared to be floating in the filthy water.

It was late afternoon, and by now everyone was aware of the scale of the disaster: the tens of thousands evacuated, the highways washed out, the still-uncertain death toll. But seeing the Stampede grounds, Lindsay Park, Victoria Park, Erlton all deluged was shocking: a powerful image of the extent of the flood.

Steve was friends with one of the assistant stage managers for the Grandstand, a choreographed big-budget musical and variety show that runs each night of the Stampede following the chuckwagon races. Still taking in the devasta-tion, he called his friend and left a voicemail: So, I'm up on the hill, and I see your stage. It's underwater... It's... um... I guess you guys could go for a pirate theme this year...

The comments drew some chuckles from the group, but it was humour as a coping mechanism. Flooding on this scale in a city this size was unprecedented in Canada; it looked like CGI effects in a Hollywood movie. And while they wondered aloud about the fate of the Stampede in two weeks' time, they had their own affected event to salvage—much smaller in size, but only a few hours away.

The challenges were numerous, as became apparent that same day when the organizers of the Sled Island festival announced they were cancelling the remainder of the sched-ule. Many of their prime venues were in flood-threatened areas; their office in Mission was already evacuated. The music, film and visual arts festival—one of the city's largest annual events, with tens of thousands attending—had been scrambling to find replacement venues, cancelling shows when absolutely necessary. Now the disaster had left them no choice.

After walking through Erlton to survey the damage, Steve's group returned to the parkour gym, which they had offered up on social media as a shelter for any evacuees. No one turned up on the doorstep, but they hunkered down with blankets and pizza and a movie, waiting. It was all they could do for now.

MEWATA ARMOURY IS ONE OF THE most recognizable buildings in the city. Completed at the end of the First World War, the red brick and sandstone Gothic Revival structure looks strikingly like a medieval castle in Calgary's Downtown West End. Its distinctive towers and buttresses and turrets are nestled between far less imposing landmarks: a light rail station and an outdoor skateboard park.

This was the headquarters of the Calgary Highlanders; but, like the rest of downtown, it was under an evacuation order, so the reservists gathered at Currie Barracks, the erstwhile location of CFB Calgary, which closed in 1998. Portions of the base had been redeveloped into residential areas with townhouses and shopping centres, but the section on the west side of Crowchild Trail was still home to the majority of full-time military personnel in the city, including Area Support Unit (ASU) Calgary, and major equipment and vehicles stores. When Sean arrived, he found his second-in-command fulfilling his leadership role in his absence. Sean was briefed and then took command of his soldiers.

There was little to do but wait and see if and when they would be called into action. Some soldiers played cards. Many watched the news, particularly those whose own homes were under threat; a few had evacuated their own families from soon-to-be-flooded areas only hours before reporting for duty. Sean, a geologist in his civilian life, spent much of the evening pouring over maps to identify potential trouble areas along the river that could be at risk for erosion. It was a small way to familiarize himself with the situation, to try and predict where they might be deployed, to be as prepared as possible when the time came to lead.

Around three o'clock in the morning, he and the others went to sleep, leaving only a few posted sentries and a staff officer waiting by the phone.

IN THE EVENING, A NUMBER OF staff volunteered to spend the night in each Trinity Place building to attend to the residents and ensure their safety while the power was out. The others went home to get some sleep. Lawrence stayed until quite late, then headed home to get what rest he could.

Stressed by the uncertainty of what was happening, Sam called her aunt again. They had spoken several times that day, but now Sam broke down. Hang up the phone, said her aunt, I'm going to call 9-1-1 and tell them you need to be evacuated. Sam hung up. A few minutes later she called back, and her aunt told her to get ready; the fire department was coming for her.

Sam called her sister, who said she could come stay with her. But for now, Sam had to wait. Though she had renewed hope of an evacuation, the timeline was not any more clear than before. By eleven o'clock it was too dark to see in the building. Sam gave up and went to bed. Maybe they'll come tomorrow.

But no sooner had she laid down than there was a knock at her door: it was the fire department, and they were there to get her out. Sam put her cat in its kennel and took that along with the small duffel bag she had packed earlier. The firemen offered to carry her down the stairs, but she refused; she wasn't comfortable with the idea of being carried unless it was absolutely necessary. Instead, they carried her bag, cat and wheelchair while Sam bummed down four flights of concrete stairs.

Once outside the building, Sam was surprised to see activity. There were people, many more than she could see from the windows above. There were residents and Trinity staff and emergency personnel. Sam could overhear a discussion about which residents were to be evacuated that night.

She was out of the building. Now she had to wait to be taken away from Edwards Place. Sam called her sister and told her what had happened. Emergency officials told her they wouldn't take her all the way to her sister's—we're not a taxi service, they said. She arranged a plan for her sister to pick her up at a convenience store on 16th Avenue North and Edmonton Trail.

After a long while, Sam was brought to an ambulance and helped inside, and they drove through the water down the street, stopping on Centre Street downtown. They waited for a while, though she wasn't sure why. Finally, another ambulance came and she was transferred into it, and this one took her to meet her sister on 16th Avenue North.

Her sister was already waiting when she arrived. In the panic and excitement of getting out, Sam had forgotten that her sister was pregnant, and she felt guilty having her carry her things. She took Sam to stay at her house, far away from the flooded East Village.

When Lorrie tried to go to sleep in her apartment that night—there was no floodwater on the main floor, and she felt safe to return—she found she was too wired, too wound up from the day's events. She tried closing her eyes and letting her mind shut off, but it was no use. Every little sound she heard worried her. What about looters? What if someone breaks in? There's no security system while the power's off!

With a flashlight in hand, Lorrie got up and walked around the main floor. There was nothing. She went for a walk on some of the other floors, but all was as it should be. She resigned herself to not sleeping and went and sat in the front lobby by the windows, waiting for morning to come.

———————————

OVER THE COURSE OF FRIDAY, a steady stream of Siksika evacuees had arrived at the Deerfoot Sportsplex. Louise and the other staff members were fighting small battles everywhere, largely of two different sorts: emotional and logistical. By the evening, there were over two hundred evacuees registered at the relief centre, and dozens of volunteers and staff. Louise stayed until the early hours of the morning before going home, physically and emotionally exhausted. She would only get a few short hours of sleep before returning.

The rivers of southern Alberta were surging to frightening new levels. Between Thursday and Saturday, many river volume records would be shattered. The all-time peak flow for the Bow River in Banff was set in 1923 at 399 m³/s. In 2012, it was recorded at 268 m³/s. It would reach 439 m³/s that weekend. In Calgary, the 2005 flood—which was the worst level of flooding many people in 2013 had expected—saw the Bow reach 791 m³/s. On Friday afternoon, it peaked at 1,740 m³/s, topping even the highest recorded figure of 1,520 m³/s set during the flood of 1932.

ON FRIDAY, THE BODY OF AMBER RANCOURT was found by her husband Scott. They had been camping near the Highwood River Thursday when the river began to rise. Scott led their horse to safety, but was hit by a wall of water and unable to make his way back to their trailer. She was thirty-five; July 30 would have been their two-year wedding anniversary.

On Friday, the body of Dominic Pearce was found. The High River man and two friends had been using a boat to try and reach a higher point of land during the flood when it capsized. The two friends were able to hang on, but Pearce lost his grip and was swept away. He was fifty-two, with an eleven-year-old son.

On Friday, the body of Jacqui Brocklebank was found. She had left her safe High River condominium to help a friend in a flooded part of town, disregarding her own cerebral palsy. She was thirty-three.

On Friday, the body of Robert Nelson was found in Okotoks. He had been working long hours on Thursday to sandbag vulnerable areas, not finishing until early Friday morning. He went home to nap, checked on the sump pump running at his home, and then went out on his ATV to check on the sandbags before dawn. He was found next to his ATV, the engine still idling, with a fatal head injury inflicted by the pavement after the vehicle rolled. He was forty-one, married with six children.

SATURDAY

While Gary slept, the temporary shelter at the former hotel was a beehive of activity. People arrived with all sorts of donations. Many of the Drop-In Centre evacuees helped them unload their vehicles, a role they often filled at the regular shelter as volunteers in the loading dock. The swimming pool and hot tub, long drained of water, were used as storage areas for donations, and were quickly filled up. A television in the lobby tuned to the news kept everyone abreast of the worsening situation in Calgary and elsewhere.

Though the response from the surrounding community was overwhelmingly supportive, the DI managers were keenly aware of the public relations challenge posed by the sudden temporary shelter. There was still some opposition and concern regarding the future use of the hotel as affordable housing, partly because some people feared the worst stereotypes of homelessness invading their community. The DI had long insisted they would not turn the building into a shelter; now they had, if only temporarily. As a precaution, the police were asked by the DI to increase their presence in the area, and several bicycle units patrolled regularly during the displacement.

The building could not be controlled as strictly as in the regular shelter, which is equipped with computer databases and digital fingerprint scanners. Here, there was no choice but to accept everyone who needed shelter. Over the next few days, however, the numbers of clients actually dropped; DI staff attributed it to long-standing familial disputes or tensions being put aside during the crisis, and clients being invited back to their homes or to stay with family and friends.

The atmosphere was positive and upbeat. Most of the clients were excited or amused by their situation. The donations continued non-stop, and someone said it was better than the actual Drop-In Centre, all this free pizza and free stuff. Private rooms would naturally pose a large security risk, so clients slept on mats on the floor in the large banquet rooms. The private rooms were opened on a strictly controlled basis for showering. Portable toilets were donated by a private company.

All this went on as Gary slept. Physical and mental exhaustion, combined with a sleep disorder, had caused him to crash hard. He finally awoke at eleven o'clock Saturday morning, having slept for nearly a full day. After using the bathroom and getting his bearings, he sat down in the lobby and watched the news on television. The full extent of the flood dawned on him for the first time.

He ate a small meal and then left, walking along a pathway beside Nose Creek—normally a peaceful trickle, now swollen into a small, forceful river—and kept walking until he approached downtown, then turned west and walked to Crescent Road overlooking the river. There were many spectators and news crews there as well, all for the same reason: normally one of the most beautiful views of the city, it was now an incredible flooded panorama of Sunnyside and downtown.

Though he was grateful to have had somewhere to go during the crisis, Gary's prejudices and discomfort about the DI clients persisted. He resolved not to go back, and he set his mind to thinking of other accommodations. Eventually, he called a friend who lived near Westbrook Mall; he was invited, and stayed there for two weeks.

THERE IS A COMMONLY USED PHRASE that has its roots in military parlance: Hurry up and wait. It refers to a situation where one is urged to complete a task quickly so as to begin waiting as soon as possible for the next step. This was the situation the Highlanders found themselves in Saturday morning.

Rising before dawn, they ate, dressed and prepared their vehicles with practised efficiency. They were ready to go, able to deploy immediately. Now they had to wait. And wait. Wait for a phone call telling them where to go and what to do, or a phone call telling them to stand down. Wait for more information, which came in at a snail's pace. They could all see the devastation on television, and the people in need of help. They were ready, able, and willing; now they had to be patient.

Word came that there was a flooded power station that needed to be saved, and that troops might be sent to sandbag. It seemed they would finally be put to use; but an hour later, the word came that the power station was a loss.

There was another power station near Deerfoot Trail that might need help, and once again the Highlanders braced themselves. But then another call came: the entire company was being deployed to Inglewood.

In an instant, the wheels were set in motion and the military machine began to move. Nearly one hundred soldiers climbed into several large utility trucks, moving out as a convoy. They drove east on Glenmore Trail, exiting the freeway at Blackfoot Trail and heading north to 19th Street Southeast, just before the Bow River crossing. This was the easternmost section of Inglewood, past the oldest parts of the city, past the trendy main drag, past the old brewery, separated from all of this by the railway tracks under which 9th Avenue dips. Here was a gas station and a charming truck stop diner. A huge parking lot provided ample room for big rigs; but today it would be used to stage a military operation.

Sean and the two other platoon leaders met with the company commander for orders. Each platoon was given a block in the small area of homes east of 19th Street Southeast. The homes were under a mandatory evacuation order, but there were still many residents who had not left. The

Highlanders' role would be to go door to door and inform residents of the order. They would make note of every response, every refusal, every empty house.

You are here for information only, they were told. You cannot force people to leave. You are not here to enforce the order.

Sean went into the gas station and bought all the city maps on the rack. He distributed them to some of his soldiers, and briefed them on their orders: their platoon was responsible for 7th Avenue and 8th Avenue. With that, they headed out on foot, walking the two blocks to the area they were charged with. The three section commanders in his platoon had radios, and Sean had a radio signaller with him. Information was constantly relayed and written down.

The easternmost portions of 7th and 8th Avenues overlook the Bow as it flows south under Blackfoot Trail before turning east. At this bend, the extremely high and fast river was causing severe erosion along the bank in front of the homes.

Some residents told the soldiers who knocked on their doors that they were staying because they didn't think the situation was that bad. One couple said they were afraid the pump keeping the water in their basement to a minimum might shut down if they left. Several people said they were worried about looting.

Sean had a geologist's perspective. He knew the river was still rising and the houses would likely collapse if the water got far enough.

He attempted to persuade people to leave using his

professional rather than military credentials: Listen, I'm in uniform right now, but I'm also a geologist. This looks like a bad situation, and you really don't need to be here. He was able to convince at least two people this way, and they packed their things and left. Many others, though, insisted on remaining.

One of the already-evacuated homes belonged to the relatives of a sergeant in Sean's platoon. He called his inlaws, who were pleased to hear that it was still standing.

After an hour and a half, the Highlanders had covered the entire area and reassembled at the truck stop. Sean and the other officers met with the police to give them the information the soldiers had collected: who had left, who was staying, which homes were empty. Meanwhile, other police officers were busy blocking off streets to make way for large flatbed trucks carrying jersey barriers and sandbags.

The company commander ordered two platoons back to ASU to await the next call; Sean's men were to remain in Inglewood.

THE PSYCHOLOGICAL IMPACT OF the flood was plain to see. Louise had observed it up close from the beginning; indeed, she had suffered herself as she bore the brunt of the stories washing over her, a sort of second-hand emotional trauma.

Beginning Saturday, her staff of crisis workers began working their regular shifts at the Siksika evacuation centre rather that at their office. A station was set up for this purpose, and they counselled victims and evaluated the mental toll exacted on them by the disaster.

Also on Saturday, an official press release was put out quoting Chief Fred Rabbit Carrier. The flood had hit the reserve only a few hours after Calgary, but the media attention had been extremely sparse thus far. The focus was primarily on the city and High River, both of which were making international headlines.

The effect of the press release was slow but steady. Social media began to spread the word that Siksika was devastated. Calls for donations were echoed online. By the end of the day, stories were posted on mainstream media sites about the losses at Siksika, with the chief's press release line quoted in all of them: "I've never seen anything like this in my life. It's very stressful. The worst I've ever seen, it's devastating."

Varkour Day was not an event on the level of Sled Island. There would not be huge crowds or line-ups. A mention in the mainstream media would be considered a coup. But it had taken months of planning and coordination; venues and schedules had been arranged, travel plans had been booked. The flood presented challenges, but the organizers cared about what they had tried to create and they were determined to try and salvage it.

Steve posted a detailed note on social media in the early morning hours of Saturday explaining how the flood would affect Varkour Day. The morning events would be unchanged, as they were scheduled to be held at the gym in the south of the city. The participants were then intended to head downtown for outdoor jam sessions at various locations. But Century Gardens in the southwest corner of downtown was the only venue not under mandatory evacuation orders.

Steve and the other organizers worried that there might be a terribly low turnout, perhaps as low as a tenth of the originally expected fifty. But twenty people—mostly women and girls—turned up at the gym, and the workshop was a great success. Some of the women had tried parkour before, but many were rookies. They learned about the philosophy of parkour, about techniques and stretching, and they had the opportunity to practice under the watchful eye of experienced coaches.

Around two o'clock in the afternoon, it was time to head downtown. Everyone piled into a few vehicles to carpool to Century Gardens. Steve stayed behind for a few minutes to help Matt and Frankie tidy the gym for classes the following morning. Then he left in his car, and they followed not far behind.

ON SATURDAY MORNING, LORRIE and another staff member went out to buy more propane for the barbecue at Edwards Place. Lorrie was greatly frustrated that the water was low enough for them to drive west on 9th Avenue in nothing more than a civilian truck, yet there still had been no evacuation. There had been no power in the building since Friday afternoon, and the authorities had not given a timeline for rescuing the hundreds of elderly and disabled residents of the three Trinity Place towers in the East Village.

When they returned with propane, they had to stop at a checkpoint and explain to the police who they were and why they were driving into the flood zone. They were allowed in unchallenged, which gave Lorrie an idea. She began telling residents to call their families to come pick them up if possible. If they come from the west, down 9th Avenue, they'll be able to get in, no problem. That's the best way to get everyone out of here right now.

But she soon heard otherwise. Residents' family members were being stopped at the police checkpoint; some got through, but others were turned away. One woman called Lorrie when she was denied access. She put the officer on the phone. The officer, apparently, was not aware that there were still people in the East Village buildings.

We aren't evacuated, we need people to be able to come

here to pick up their families! We have no power and we need to get people out!

What I can tell you, ma'am, is that you should call our dispatch and inform them of your situation.

They should already know we're here! And, anyway, why can't you do that? I mean, they're going to listen to you more than they'll listen to me.

Well, I suggest you give them a call and explain your situation to them if you need people to be able to get into the flood zone.

Nothing was resolved. The officer would not let the woman through. But calling the police dispatch would have been redundant: Trinity Place executives had been lobbing calls at city officials for days, a practice that only increased in frequency and urgency when the power went out completely. Lawrence managed to get through to CEMA and spoke to someone in a senior position. He reiterated their frustration with the situation, the previous assurances from emergency officials, and the many vulnerable people who were trapped in a building without power.

And then it happened. Beginning around four o'clock, the fire, police, and EMS departments, along with Trinity staff, began the long process of bringing residents out of Edwards Place and the two other buildings. City buses were brought in to transport the evacuees to their temporary shelters. Most went to the Southland Leisure Centre, but others were sent to private care facilities as dictated by their needs and the limited spaces available.

Most of the residents, though elderly, were able to walk out under their own power with assistance from emergency workers or other staff. Lights were needed in the darkened stairwells, and the process was slow and cautious.

Not everything went smoothly. Over at King Tower, Lawrence butted heads with senior emergency officials. Lorrie heard a story of one elderly woman being helped with her suitcases down the stairs of Edwards Place by a fire-fighter, only to have him leave her suddenly—I have to go, I'll be right back. The woman waited, but no one came back. She carried down what she could by herself. It wasn't until later that someone discovered her remaining bags and returned them to her.

But these were exceptions in a stressful time, and the emergency workers were largely friendly and professional. Lorrie helped escort residents out of the building. She and other staff marked empty suites with an X to simplify the evacuation. When the final bus departed for the leisure centre at around nine o'clock that night, she followed behind it in her van to reassure all the displaced tenants that they weren't abandoned.

SEAN WAS ALMOST LITERALLY born to be a soldier. His father had been a reservist for thirty-five years. His grandfather served before him. His great-grandfather fought in the Second World War, his great-great-grandfather fought in the First World War, and his great-great-great grandfather was a British soldier who came to Canada to help put down the second Riel rebellion in 1885; he stayed in Canada after he was offered free land.

Sean grew up in Hamilton and joined the reserves as soon as he was eligible, within six months of his seventeenth birthday. He remained in the reserves for four years, then joined the regular forces to serve in a peacekeeping mission to Bosnia in 2001.

Two notable events took place while Sean was overseas. One was his twenty-first birthday; the other was 9/11. The latter event was a frantic and stressful day to be an active soldier in a foreign country. Radio calls ordered his unit back to base immediately; alert states suddenly went to the highest possible level. Back at the base, Sean watched CNN with the others, aghast and mesmerized like the rest of the world, certain they were going to war. Against who? Who knows. But this is it.

Instead, Sean found himself back in Canada at the end of his tour the following month. He began an undergraduate program at McMaster University and rejoined the reserves. When Canada pledged troops to the NATO mission in Afghanistan, he decided not to join. He felt he'd fulfilled his duty and now needed to focus on other priorities.

Sean proved to be a natural leader, and he reached the rank of warrant officer at a relatively young age. When he moved west in 2010 to begin his masters in geology at the

University of Calgary, he joined the Highlanders and was soon asked to take his commission and become a lieutenant.

The process required retaking many of the standard military tests given to new recruits: aptitude exams, word association exercises, basic math, a lengthy physical fitness test, and an interview with a selection officer. In all, it took Sean a year and a half to become a commissioned officer.

He was a good fit for the added responsibility. Sean loved the thrill of firing rocket launchers and throwing grenades in training exercises as much as any other soldier. But he also recognized the importance of keeping his paperwork in order to make life easier for his platoon members. Office work for him was no less important to his job than physical fitness; it was all about competence, discipline, focus. Wanting to do it doesn't enter into the equation; it is a job that must be done, and done well. This strong sense of duty helped Sean keep the younger members of his platoon focused in Inglewood. At least half of the Highlanders had served in Afghanistan, more than any other reserve corps in the country; knocking on doors and asking people to leave fell well short of the adrenaline rush of combat.

The erosion was getting worse. City engineers and contractors were hoping to stave it off by deflecting the force of the water with concrete jersey barriers and sandbags. A massive flatbed truck and trailer loaded with sandbags was parked on the street near the most extreme erosion. Sean approached a man in a white helmet who appeared to be in charge.

I've got thirty-five young, strong backs. How can I help? The man's face beamed. Really? Oh, that's amazing!

The man, who worked for a city contractor, wanted to get the many jersey barriers into the water as quickly as possible to halt the erosion. But the huge sandbag truck had arrived first and was blocking the other trucks.

The solution was to move the sandbag truck around the corner onto 22nd Street, allowing the other trucks access. While the jersey barriers were installed, the Highlanders began unloading the sandbags by hand into a front-end loader, which then dropped them near the water to be placed. There were thousands of sandbags, and it was exhausting work.

THE VARKOUR DAY CARPOOLERS KNEW Macleod Trail was closed around downtown, so they headed north on Crowchild. Steve exited onto 17th Avenue South, then headed north on 14th Street West. Blockades were appearing at intersections, an ominous sign, though his route had not yet been closed off. Steve turned down 10th Avenue South and headed east. At the 8th Street subway, which dips under the CP tracks and 9th Avenue into downtown, he found a large dump truck parked sideways to block the road. He parked and walked the two blocks through the subway to Century Gardens.

There he found the group of about ten or so who had come in the first two cars. They had been able to drive right up to the park when they arrived fifteen minutes earlier, and they were busy practising parkour on the concrete structures. Mosquitos were everywhere. Steve called the other drivers for a report. Matt and Frankie had been turned away from the area, even though they were just a couple minutes behind Steve. Presumably it would be the same situation for the other cars.

The sky was beginning to darken as Steve walked over to a nearby hotel and asked the staff if they had any information about the status of the area. Some emergency workers happened to come in, and they answered Steve's question: the area was now under a voluntary evacuation; they didn't have to leave, but they were strongly encouraged to.

Steve called the other organizers and discussed a new plan. Another popular parkour spot was at the Southern Alberta Institute of Technology, up on North Hill. The only question was if the bridges were open to cross the river. Matt and Frankie said they would head over there. Steve walked back to the group at Century Gardens and gave them the new plan. They got into their cars and headed for SAIT while Steve walked back to 10th Avenue.

The plan fell apart sooner than he could get to his car. It was a chaotic mess, with people texting and phoning each other, drivers unable to answer while driving, uncertainty and misinformation being spread around. In the end, it was decided to simply gather everyone back at the gym. Some still ended up at SAIT; others simply went home after being turned away from downtown. Instead of the trendy bar in the Beltline that had been planned, the evening turned out to be a delicious and jovial meal at the family-run Vietnamese restaurant near the gym.

IT DIDN'T TAKE LONG FOR the media to show up in Inglewood, perhaps having caught wind of the soldiers' presence from the social media posts of nearby residents. Photographers and television crews captured the Highlanders sweating in fatigues as they heaved the sandbags under the hot June sun. Sean gave interviews, and escorted one photographer closer to the erosion.

A pair of well-known local coffee roasters showed up with complimentary coffee for the troops, and the owner of an Inglewood pizza shop brought fresh pizza on a scooter. These small gestures were greatly appreciated by the soldiers during their long, hard day.

Once the sandbags had been moved from the truck to 8th Avenue, Sean brought his entire platoon over to form a chain, passing each bag down the line from one man to the next, eventually dropping it in place along the erosion. By now, the water had chewed away the strip of grassy park that ran along it and had advanced several metres towards the houses. Because the river, even in its swollen state, was nearly two metres below the level of the road, it had eroded the earth beneath the pavement, causing the road to crack and crumble without sufficient support. It was around ten o'clock with sunset nearing when the job was done. Tired and sweaty, the Highlanders piled into their trucks and headed back to Currie Barracks for a short night's sleep.

SUNDAY

The list of severe urban floods in major Canadian cities is a short one. In 1954, a storm caused by Hurricane Hazel and dubbed Hazel II inundated Toronto with heavy rain, raising river levels by six to eight metres and causing massive flooding in the western areas of Greater Toronto. The flood primarily affected low, flat farmland and areas along the Humber River rather than the urban city itself, but the devastation was enormous: roads, houses and farms were washed away; over four thousand families were rendered homeless overnight; eighty-one people were killed, and it stands to this day as the deadliest natural disaster in Canadian history.

In 1987, Montreal was hit with over 100 millimetres of rainfall in less than three hours. Sewer systems were not able to cope, and roads across the island city were flooded. The Décarie Expressway, which is sunken several metres below ground level as it cuts across the island, quickly filled with water, trapping motorists who needed to be rescued by firefighters. One man drowned in his car; another was electrocuted.

The Red and Assiniboine Rivers have often threatened Winnipeg—most notably in 1950 and 1997—and have caused widespread devastation in other areas. But when a quarter of the city was flooded in 1950, Winnipeg was far smaller and less developed than 21ˢᵗ century Calgary.

Skyscrapers, each with basements full of operational infrastructure; dozens of condominiums and office towers with heaters and boilers and elevator equipment; light-rail tunnels, freeways, public art installations, and expansive modern park developments—these hardly existed, if at all, in 1950 Winnipeg or 1954 Toronto, while Montreal's flood lasted only a few hours and caused a fraction of the damage seen in Calgary. Even the public infrastructure damages alone put the cost of the flood in Calgary into the billions; the business and residential losses would be similarly enormous.

On Sunday morning, Ritch was watching the news on television when he saw a shot of Bow Crescent. There was evident activity on the street behind the reporter. People were there. There hadn't been any official announcement of the evacuation order lifting, but Ritch decided it was worth a try.

Driving towards Bow Crescent, he saw police but no barricades, no one stopping him or others from driving right up to their homes. There was still some water on the road, but it had gone down enough to allow ordinary cars to pass.

Their yard was muddy and dirty, covered with silt and randomly strewn objects, only some of which he recognized. Ritch entered the house and breathed a sigh of great relief: there was no apparent water damage on the main floor. The basement, however, still had six feet of water in it. Books floated near the ceiling. But the water had stopped short of the main crossbeam, which would have brought a much larger and more expensive set of problems.

Ritch called his wife and told her to come down to the house. Then he went out and sat on the front step and watched the street. His neighbours, only some of whom he knew, were getting started with salvage; but no one really seemed confident in what they were doing. They looked as Ritch felt, bewildered, overwhelmed. Where to start? What to do? How to manage and prioritize? How does one begin?

A pickup truck came with a barbecue on the back, and a man hollered to everyone within earshot that he was grilling free hamburgers and hot dogs for anyone who wanted to eat. Slowly, some residents began to walk over, shellshocked, looking like zombies.

THE MEDIA ATTENTION WAS a turning point for the relief effort at Siksika. Until then, the reserve had been more or less on its own. Donations and volunteers were coming almost entirely from the Nation itself. But on Sunday, the trucks began arriving.

Initially, the donated items—clothes, food, supplies—were piled in the lobby of the arena section of the sportsplex. But the trucks kept coming with donations; a line of them snaked along the road leading up to the building, backed up nearly to the highway at one point. There was no ice in the arena, so the donations were moved there, and they gradually filled the space.

The donations came from individuals, charities, cultural groups, businesses and religious organizations. They came from the cities and towns. They came from other First Nations. The staff at the sportsplex did their best to record the source of each donation, which was not an easy task at the rate they were arriving.

Phones were ringing off the hook. There were two women working the reception desk, and it seemed that for every call they answered, two more lines would ring with calls waiting. Louise's cell phone was rarely quiet as individuals and organizations rang to ask what sort of things were needed.

One cultural group who had come from Calgary asked Louise what they could provide. The arena was fast filling with the obvious items, like clothes and food and diapers.

You know what we need? A better way to communicate. I'm running all over the place trying to go between the arena and the gymnasium and all the stations. I can't be everywhere at once.

In short order, the staff were equipped with wireless radios, smoothing the operation of the relief centre.

Not all donations were in the form of goods. Many people and groups sent money and gift cards. Louise gave strict instructions that she be called immediately when such things came in. She locked them in the office, wearing the only key around her neck. The fewer hands on cash donations, the better, especially in the midst of so much chaos.

A great amount of help came from the Hutterites, who arrived several dozen strong from the nearby colony and went straight to work at Siksika. The women helped in the kitchen, cleaning and serving food. The men unloaded donations from the trucks with great speed. They're like ants, someone remarked to Louise. They're just so... organized. And they never stop working.

Several groups of people had opted to leave the evacuation centre and camp outside, both to get away from the crowds and to be on the hills overlooking their flooded homes. Many of them had tents and trailers of their own, but others were inquiring about them, and Louise added tents to the list of donation requests.

Because the two bridges spanning the Bow River on the reserve were both badly damaged—one had an entire span washed away—and the one at Carseland was also closed, the fastest way to drive to the south shore of the reserve was to go west into Calgary, then south to Okotoks and back east again: at least two hours, depending on traffic in the city. Since people were camping on the far shore, Merlin ordered a truck of supplies be driven out to them to lessen the burden of having to return regularly to the sportsplex.

The media came in the afternoon, and the chief gave an outdoor press conference and one-on-one interviews. The cameras captured the flooded reserve and the crowded sportsplex. The evening newscasts and the Monday papers would show the public what had happened to the reserve. On Monday, a helicopter would film footage of the widespread devastation for a national newspaper. The stories and incredible images would keep the donations and volunteers coming in droves.

THE HIGHLANDERS ROSE AGAIN at five o'clock Sunday morning. In short order they were fed, dressed and packed, and some time around seven Sean's platoon arrived at the Inglewood Community Centre. Their mission for the day was decidedly unthrilling: they would serve as information officers for displaced residents wanting to know about their houses, and about what would come next.

The City had begun distributing pamphlets about proper safety procedures for reentering homes; what to do if the water line is above the lowest electrical outlet, for example. Handing out this information became the primary task of these highly trained soldiers.

As the residents came in and spoke to the Highlanders, Sean soon took notice of something. Despite the evacuation order still in effect, many people had gone to look at their homes; others, in the areas without any direct threat of flooding, had never left. Some were without electricity, some were without gas, and many had neither.

This potential for intelligence gathering was not lost on the lieutenant. Sean procured a large map of Inglewood from the community centre, detailed down to the lot of each house. The soldiers thus transformed their mission to include information gathering as well as distribution.

Each resident who came in was asked if they knew the status of their house. If they did, the information was plotted on the map, to be later shared with the power and gas companies, facilitating the restoration of utility service in the coming days.

Many people wanted more answers than the soldiers could give. When will the power be back on? When will the evacuation order be lifted? When will we be allowed back home?

We don't know.

Then why are you here?

Several homeowners came in asking about their homes on 8th Avenue, where the Highlanders had been sandbagging the previous day. The residents knew how real the threat was there, and the concern on their faces was obvious as they asked if their homes were okay. Sean grinned as he pulled out his smart phone and showed them the pictures he'd taken of the area that morning while getting updated by the police. Yeah, here's your house right here! Totally fine!

In the afternoon, Sean was told to send one of his three sections to the neighbouring community of Ramsay, where the soldiers would serve much the same role at the community centre there. Residents in Ramsay were allowed to return home already, and there was less frustration from those who came in.

In Inglewood, people were making the best of things. Those who were without power brought in their refrigerated food that was in danger of spoiling, and it was pooled together for a community barbecue. A soccer game started on the pitch and the soldiers joined in when their work was slow.

Do you think we should go easy and let them win?

Sean grinned. No way, play hard!

The score was hardly important, though. The community where Calgary had been born had escaped largely unscathed from the threat of disaster, and even though kids were playing soccer against soldiers in fatigues, it felt very much like an ordinary summer day.

ON SUNDAY, THE BODY OF Lorraine Gerlitz was found by friends in her ground-level Erlton apartment. She had been aware of the mandatory evacuation order, and told both friends and officials that she intended to leave. Her family described her as clear-thinking and physically able, and her reasons for staying were a mystery. Hers was the fifth and final confirmed death related to the floods. She was eighty-three.

NAHEED NENSHI WAS ELECTED as the thirty-sixth mayor of Calgary in 2010, assuming office October 25. His victory made news headlines around the world, much to his bemusement, as he was the first Muslim elected as mayor of a major North American city—a fact that was largely either celebrated by Calgarians or dismissed with refreshingly genuine indifference.

He was not projected to win: two household-name candidates, one a long-time alderman, the other a long-time news anchor, were the heavyweights in the race. Nenshi's campaign of unusually intelligent and honest dialogue on serious issues, and especially his use of social media to engage young voters, was held up and examined by political experts and the media following his win. Calgary's tradition of electing rather liberal mayors clashes with its popular image as a conservative city, and Nenshi's victory especially baffled many in the rest of the country.

The young mayor, thirty-eight when elected, was a born charmer. His distinctive mildly-nasal voice, his often unruly dark curls, his plumpish figure, his easy grin and goofy laugh, his forever-slipping rectangular spectacles, his affable personality and penchant for self-deprecation—whatever your politics, he was hard to dislike. Styling himself as a pragmatic centrist more interested in common sense than rigid ideology, the mayor's signature campaign colour of purple combined the blue and red of the federal Conservatives and Liberals.

The social media savvy he displayed during his election campaign continued in his mayoralty. He mastered Twitter like few politicians ever can, engaging with his many fans and fewer but vocal foes daily. Nenshi could be sentimental, snarky, funny, serious, intelligent—whatever the moment called for. He rarely struck a bad chord with his fans online. He soon soared passed the 100,000 followers mark. To compare, Rahm Emanuel, the mayor of Chicago and former White House chief of staff, had around 70,000. In short, Nenshi was a star.

The beloved mayor was the face of his city, and when the flood hit, his social media acumen was indispensible. His legions of followers looked to the civic leader himself for updates. During the crisis, his Twitter handle would be mentioned 89,000 times. By comparison, Stephen Harper's handle would be mentioned 22,800 times; Premier Alison Redford, a distant 8,000.

The mayor's seemingly bottomless energy and dedication was noted and praised, and the hashtags #Nap4Nenshi and #NapForNenshi were used over 4,200 times in a campaign to convince the man to take a well-deserved break. Citizens playfully scolding their elected leaders for working too hard during an unfolding emergency is not a well-documented phenomenon.

On Sunday, with the rivers still dangerously high and the disaster not yet over, Nenshi addressed the city in a televised press conference. In a stern deadpan, he spoke: I can't believe I actually have to say this, but I'm going to say it: the river is closed. You cannot boat on the river. I have a large number of nouns that I can use to describe the people I saw in a canoe on the Bow River today. I am not allowed to use any of them. I can tell you, however, that I have been told that, despite the state of local emergency, I'm not allowed to invoke the Darwin law. If you are on the river we have to rescue you. If we have to rescue you we're taking away valuable resource from others. Every time we have to pull a rescue boat onto the river, it means there is not a rescue boat in a community that is flooded. It is selfish and it is ridiculous for you to be on the river. So, do not do it.

The admonishing speech went viral online and was widely replayed and reprinted. The hashtag #NenshiNoun began trending. The mayor's image as a political leader of above-average likeability, competence and intelligence had grown during the flood into something more. Politicians often see their polling numbers rise during and after a disaster when recovery goes reasonably well, but Nenshi had somehow become a folk hero.

Once again, his name and face were in the news far beyond Alberta. Most people in Vancouver or Toronto would likely be hard-pressed to name any Calgary mayor previous to him; even Ralph Klein is more widely remembered as premier than mayor. But Nenshi was suddenly mononymically famous, and even his staunchest political opponents joined in praising his crisis leadership.

RECOVERY

E arly Monday morning, CEMA officials issued a public call for volunteers. A strategy had been formulated that went against an accepted tenent of emergency response management: rather than wait for the crisis to fully subside in all areas before beginning recovery efforts, officials wanted to quickly get as many people cleaning up their homes as possible, where safe to do so.

Part of this meant distributing pamphlets with information for residents returning to their houses. The statement released Monday morning asked for citizens looking to help to meet at McMahon Stadium in a few hours. They were hoping for around six hundred people to assist with reentry. But the request was promptly shared and re-shared on social media, and city officials were shocked to find three thousand people swarming the stadium parking lot by ten o'clock, many of them clad in rubber boots hoping to be deployed to flood-affected areas.

There was no plan for this level of turnout. Officials scrambled to find more jobs and assignments for the volunteers, many of whom had to be turned away. Some of them were told to simply drive in their own vehicles to community reception centres and ask what help was needed. Others realized the City wasn't looking for people willing to get their hands dirty and went off on their own to find roles to fill.

There were many people in Calgary who were unaffected by the floods, who wanted to lend a hand, who had time to spare with their offices telling them to stay home. The desire to help was everywhere. What was needed was direction.

THERE WAS MUCH MORE ACTIVITY on Bow Crescent when Ritch and Cathy returned Monday morning. It seemed the entire neighbourhood had returned to begin the clean-up process. Volunteers had begun appearing in groups, strangers looking to help any way they could.

Everything was a mess. The foremost problem for Ritch and Cathy, aside from the filthy silt and muck in the yard and garage, was the many feet of water still in the basement. The first order of business was finding a pump—not a simple task in a city cleaning itself up from a massive flood.

The mess overwhelmed Cathy. It was difficult to process, to see the steps through which everything could gradually be dealt with. What should be done first? The basement needed work, but nothing could be done until the water was pumped out, so perhaps the yard, but where to start?

A group of two men and two women in their twenties

came walking down Bowbank Crescent and approached their property. Do you need help? Instinctively, Cathy said no. Check with the people in this house over here, they've got young kids.

One of the women in the group stepped forward and said to Cathy: You need help, too. It's okay. Cathy looked at her and realized how lost she felt with the outsized task before them. You're right. Thank you.

They came around to the front of the house. The group had been helping a friend of theirs who lived just around the corner on Bowbank Crescent, right along the river. There was still so much water in his house that only the garage was ready for work. Having finished cleaning it out, they were now moving from house to house offering to help. The first house they tried was already overwhelmed with volunteers; the second was not ready for help; and the third was Ritch and Cathy's.

One of the group, Dan, asked Ritch: What can we help with?

I don't know where to start.

Well, how's your garage look?

No, no, don't go in there! There's no power to open the big door, and the floor is thick with mud and gunk. It's a real mess. Dan smiled. Well, that's why we're here. Don't worry, we'll get it open.

Dan entered through the side door of the garage, walking through the disgusting accumulation of filth and waste deposited by the river. From the inside, he was able to open the main door. The four volunteers—Dan, his girlfriend Meera, his sister and her friend—spent hours cleaning it out. Other volunteers joined throughout the day, moving on to the backyard after the garage was finished.

The street was bustling with activity: people sweeping, scrubbing, scraping their properties, hauling out ruined items from the basements that had drained, pumping out those that had not. As the work progressed, so did the noise; but it was reassuring noise, the sound of a living neighbourhood.

It was hard to know when it was time to quit for the day. The job certainly wasn't finished, and though everyone was tired and filthy, there was such an energy that many people kept working past the supper hour. But at some point, sensing the end of the day was near, Ritch decided he wanted to say something.

The volunteers working in his yard stopped to listen to him as he did his best to thank them. He was an outgoing man not normally lost for words, but it took some doing to find the right ones; even then, it wasn't enough to express their gratitude.

He added an offer: What I do for a living is manage a banquet centre here in Bowness. If any of you guys ever get married, you give me a call and I'll look after you. It's the least I can do.

Dan gave Meera an playful elbow jab and she rolled her eyes. Marriage? Already? Give me a break.

SEAN'S PLATOON WAS AGAIN DISPATCHED to Inglewood and Ramsay on Monday. Again the soldiers collected information on their maps, answered questions, handed out post-flood documents to residents. The rivers had long since crested, the waters were abating, and the emergency part of the crisis was over.

Despite being largely quite young, Sean's men never questioned their orders or assignments. But though they never voiced their thoughts directly, Sean sometimes sensed a group feeling that they ought to be better used, that there was surely something more that they could be doing.

He did his best to emphasize the importance of their role: See that old lady who just left knowing everything she needs to know when she goes back into her house? That's why we're here.

Sometimes, he had to be more direct: The reason we are effective in this situation is because we're an organized unit with a hierarchy that can deploy rapidly and follow orders. Guess what orders we were given.

Um, go to the community centre and pass out information?

That is correct. And that is what we are doing.

When they left Inglewood that evening, Sean's men returned to Currie Barracks. There they joined not only the rest of the Highlanders but all regiments deployed during the flood. They were gathered on a small hill on the edge of a parking lot in front of their headquarters and told to stand at ease. A large green flatbed truck holding a speaker and microphone sat in front of them. There were men standing on the truck, and one of them stepped forward and spoke.

Well, what an honour for me to address all of you today, began the mayor. I don't have a lot to say, because who wants to listen to a politician speak?

A few soldiers chuckled, and Sean decided the moment was appropriate to take a photo. He pulled out his phone and held it up as Nenshi continued.

All I want to do is just say thank-you. Thank-you to all of you— hey, does 'at ease' involve taking camera-phone pictures? They mayor gestured to Sean, picking him out of the large crowd, and the soldiers laughed as Nenshi contin-ued his speech. He thanked them for the work done in Inglewood and elsewhere. He thanked the reservists from Calgary and those who came from other place. Then he introduced Bruce Burrell—the fire chief and head of CEMA —who thanked the troops for taking the strain off city crews during the crisis.

Sean's photo opportunity notwithstanding, the men and women in the crowd were not star-struck by the closest equi-valent to a rock star in Canadian municipal politics. Though they stood at ease as they listened to the men on the truck speak, the soldiers were calm and serious, unlike the regular crowds who clambered for the mayor's autograph.

After the speeches and polite applause, Nenshi came down off the truck and walked towards the troops, engaging them on a more personal and casual level, as befitted his personal brand of politics. He thanked them again. He joked with the soldiers who had come from Yellowknife. He gave one of his staff members his phone to take a photograph as he posed with soldiers. The crowd couldn't help but smile in the face of such natural charm.

Soon Nenshi and Burrell wrapped up their visit. The troops were snapped back to attention and marched out. Though their work was done, the soldiers were required by policy to remain at the barracks overnight, lest anyone be too tired or stressed to get behind the wheel of a car.

Many of the reservists would go home Tuesday only to take off their uniform and head back out to volunteer, swapping army boots for rubber boots. Sean, though, had to focus on more pressing matters: he would defend his geology master's thesis in less than a week.

AS STEVE DROVE SOUTH ON 8th Street Southwest, down the hill from Mount Royal towards the three-way stop at 30th Avenue, he saw an abrupt change, almost like a demarcation line. Turning left into the neighbourhood of Elbow Park, then right towards his aunt and uncle's house, he was suddenly in the midst of the aftermath. Mount Royal felt ordinary, its mansions safe up on the hill; Elbow Park, along the river from which it takes its name, was a disaster zone.

It was Monday afternoon, and residents were just beginning to return to their homes and start the clean-up. Though his aunt and uncle's home was just a few blocks away, it took Steve nearly fifteen minutes to drive down 7th Street, which was cramped with trucks and people and debris. People carried pieces of their lives out of basements with a sort of grim determination, piling them for now, until the dumpsters arrived.

Steve's relatives had been hit hard by the flood, their basement submerged under two metres of water. His parents and other relations had been working all morning to clear the basement out. Now the women worked to clean salvagable items as best they could while Steve, his two uncles and his father debated how high the cut line in the drywall ought to be.

The highest areas of the walls had been untouched by the water, but moisture was wicking upwards into the dry sections. The discussion of where to cut—how much was too wasteful, how close to the moisture was too risky—would later strike Steve as emblematic of the mindset of the first days of recovery: save as much as you can, wherever you can. The drywall they left up would come down eventually, once the new wall panels were installed. The debate was meaningless, except that it filled the instinctive need to conserve what little there was left.

The men cut the drywall and bashed it out with shovels. As they worked, Steve couldn't help remembering the countless hours he'd spent in that basement with his cousins, who were the eldest of his generation of the family. They were the ones Steve looked up to and took his cues from. Those memories—when they were safe from the boring upstairs adults in their children's basement world—didn't make the work any easier.

Before he arrived at the house, Steve had posted the address on social media asking for help from anyone looking to volunteer. He soon received a response from an old friend from high school he hadn't spoken to for years. The friend was looking to help.

It was around four o'clock when Dave arrived with shovels, hammers, and a crowbar he'd borrowed from his neighbour. After a few friendly minutes of catching up with Steve and meeting his family, Dave joined in with earnest, tearing out the drywall and ripping up the flooring. He'd invited some of his own friends to join; they arrived two hours later, and the work was spread amongst them.

The mood was upbeat, if not exactly happy. Dave knew Steve to be a positive sort of person, and he saw that it ran in the family. Nobody was down and out. It was miserable work for the family, but everyone did their best to go about it with a level of stoicism and optimism. There were even jokes at times about how a flood really helps to eliminate clutter. Steve's father was teased for trying to salvage ruined items for his own house. Dad, you really need to get your house flooded. You're taking stuff out of the flooded basement!

A dumpster had been placed outside, and the workers busied themselves filling it from the piles of rubbish that had accumulated. While reaching into one pile for a handful, Dave happened to find a two dollar bill. It was a strange sight, not only because he hadn't seen one in at least a decade, but because it was in perfect condition.

He called over Steve to show him. Real nice, Dave. You come to volunteer and then you start looting.

Dave took the bill to Steve's uncle and offered it to him. No, you can keep it. You've surely earned it today.

More of Steve's friends responded to his social media call for help as the day went on, raising the total number of workers and shortening the day's work. The group continued into the evening, not stopping until the basement was gutted, the dumpster was filled, and there was nothing left.

They celebrated the day with pizza. It was around nine o'clock when everyone said their farewells. The feeling for Steve's family had been overwhelming loss at the start of the day, but it ended with overwhelming gratitude for the volunteers—strangers to them—who had done in a single day more than they could have hoped.

They had spent more than four decades in that house, but that day was one they'd never forget.

MONDAY HAD SEEN A HUM of activity as Bowness residents returned to their homes, but on Tuesday the recovery effort kicked into overdrive as Bow Crescent overflowed with volunteers. Strangers went from house to house, offering their labour.

A man from Cochrane brought four pumps for people to use. He loaned one to Ritch to empty the basement of water; the rest he set up at different houses along the street. The man spent the day continually checking on his pumps, ensuring they were running smoothly, refuelling them, moving them to other homes once a job was finished..

An older couple came by the house offering to help. They were from Burlington, Ontario, in town for the birth of their first grandson. When the floods hit, they felt compelled to come volunteer. There was an old trunk of letters and keepsakes that had been kept in the garage; the papers were fragile, wet and stuck together. The couple spent the day carefully going through the trunk and separating the letters and photographs. They placed them between paper towels to soak up the dirty water, then hung them on lines of string throughout the house.

Cathy was overwhelmed. The trunk contained irreplaceable family treasures: photographs of her father in the air force, and from her mother's time working for British intelligence during the Second World War; her mother's passport and correspondence with the Trudeaus. The strangers from the other side of the country spent hours salvaging the delicate materials simply to be kind and helpful.

Later that day, the pump draining the basement suddenly stopped. The man who owned it came over to inspect it. Must be something stuck in here, he said. I'll get it out.

With the volunteers helping and the first real signs of progress evident that day, Ritch's mood was improving. Well, if you find a diamond in there, you can keep it!

Ritch was out in the yard when a crew from a local talk radio station pulled up in front of the house. Can we ask you a few questions?

Ritch gave his answers into a microphone. The questions were all predictable. How long have you lived here? How bad is the damage? What will you do now?

The reporter thanked Ritch and put away the microphone. Hang on, said Ritch, you're not done yet. The microphone was turned back on, and he continued: You have to mention the volunteers, that's the real story. We would still be sitting on our front steps with our heads in our hands if these droves of people hadn't shown up.

The reporter thanked Ritch again and continued on down the street in search of more interviews.

Cathy was inside the house taking a rest when one of her work colleagues came to the door. Cathy invited her in and showed her the damage to the house, the yard, the water-logged basement. Her colleague burst into tears, overwhelmed by the scale of the devastation. She had brought paper towel, rubber gloves and disinfectant, expecting to help clean up a few muddy items. As she cried, Cathy found herself consoling and reassuring her. It's all right, we're doing okay.

While she was there, the colleague took photos of the property and shared them at the company business meeting;

half a dozen managers and department heads came out to volunteer the following day.

———————————

WHILE TEARING OUT HIS aunt and uncle's basement, Steve had been in touch with a friend who had been at her parents' new house in Sunnyside for her birthday the night of the flood. The party had turned into a mad rush to save things from the basement, everyone carrying furniture and belongings upstairs in a race against the water, which badly damaged the house. His friend wasn't able to help her parents on Tuesday, and she asked Steve if he could go over.

He posted the address and his phone number online and got several responses. When he arrived on Tuesday, there were already other friends and family helping, along with other volunteers. The street was busier than in Elbow Park the previous day: residents had now had a day to assess and begin clean-up, and the volunteer response was more developed. Every so often his phone would vibrate in his pocket with a message from someone looking to help.

Soon there were upwards of fifteen people at the house. The work was going quickly, though Steve's knee—still weak from recent surgery—limited his capabilities to some extent. Even if he avoided the painful tasks of lifting or shovelling, the slippery mud on the floor and stairs was dangerous and worrisome. He was determined to help with the flood clean-up, and he did his best to put the pain out of his mind.

Steve continued texting with his friend, letting her know how the job was going. She told him that a friend of hers—a single mother two blocks away—had almost no one to help her. The message was relayed and a couple of workers broke off to go assist.

Once that happened, their view of the area grew larger than just the houses in the immediate vicinity, and the volunteers realized their large crew could afford to fan out and help others. Everyone in need of assistance was very eager to have strangers come into their house and start ripping out their drywall. Introductions were brief, and names were difficult to remember. These were not important things in the face of the work to be done.

One house that received the attention of the group belonged to an elderly couple. It sat closer to the river along Memorial Drive, where the houses were more damaged than ones further north, and there seemed to be less activity and fewer workers.

The couple had a pair of elderly friends helping them, but they needed young backs and strong arms. The basement needed to be cleared but the awkward exit at the top of the stairs slowed things down greatly with a poorly designed combination of a right-angle turn, a narrow outside corridor against a fence, and a door that blocked one's path when opened. The basement window would be a more efficient way to pass out rubbish, but the security bars wouldn't budge.

The two volunteers who had come to help returned to the

house Steve was at and asked for assistance. He and another worker came and spent some time on the bars, trying to pry them off before using brute force with a sledgehammer. The work moved much more smoothly after that, and the basement began to empty. Steve stayed there working for four hours, and more people gradually joined, the fruits of his social media posting. Around eight o'clock, his knee in pain and covered in mud, Steve drove out of Sunnyside and headed home.

BY WEDNESDAY, THE WATER IN the basement had significantly decreased, thanks to the Cochrane man's pump, and Ritch and Cathy were able to go downstairs for the first time.

It was a disgusting mess. The basement had held some seven feet of floodwater for five full days. Everything was covered in filth, everything was soggy, everything stank. It was, unsurprisingly, a near-total loss. They began the long and disagreeable process of hauling things up. Volunteers came and helped, but the work was slow and difficult; for Ritch and Cathy, it was emotionally draining as well.

Cathy felt like she was losing her mind on a daily basis, living in some unreal and terrible world, like a nightmare, where she had no control over the terrible things that were happening. She felt the stress and strain wearing her down. It was hard to cope.

The pump was still running to get the last few inches of water out. The Cochrane man was around, walking between his four pumps at different houses, refuelling them and keeping them running smoothly. He stopped by Ritch and Cathy's to check their pump; it was running fine. As he was leaving, something in one of the piles of rubbish caught his eye: a Saint Christopher medal on a chain. He pulled it out, and on the end of the chain was a diamond ring.

He brought it over to Cathy, who was astounded. The ring was her mother's engagement ring, which she had given to Katie when she went to Europe. Katie had worn it to pretend she was engaged. After the trip, she'd attached it to the necklace with the Saint Christopher medal for safekeeping. It had been thrown out of the basement by someone who hadn't realized what was in the soggy pile they'd grabbed. Cathy was thrilled. She thanked the man for saving it.

The man walked around to the front of the house where Ritch was and told him the story. Then, with a crooked smile, he said: You know, you did say if I found I diamond I could keep it. I guess that deal's off. The men laughed together, a cathartic moment among the despair.

The clean-up was indeed a difficult process for all residents, but the volunteers had been wonderful and unexpected. All along the street, people were looking to help wherever they could. The work was dirty and filthy, but it had to be done; still, it was remarkable the lengths to which people were willing to go for complete strangers in need.

Monica had been volunteering in Bowness since Monday. She was a natural organizer. She was always the one to organize events, spearhead the planning for anything, or bring groups together. Whether in the community or through her son's school, Monica organized almost by default. So when Bowness began to clean itself up, she formed a group to help parents of students at her son's school, which sits near the bridge to Montgomery at the southern end of Bow Crescent.

She reached out to everyone she knew and asked them to come down. The scene on arrival had struck her as something like a war zone: the entire street was devastated, everyone was in shock. The inital task, like everywhere else, was either pumping out or tearing out the basements, depending on the level of water that remained. Dumpsters were few and far between; most people just made piles of their rubbish to deal with later. Though Monica's group initially helped the school parents as planned, there were simply too many in need, and the volunteers began to fan out among other houses.

Monica grew up in Montgomery, where her mother and father still lived. Though she wasn't a Bownesian, she saw few distinctions between the two communities. To her, they were one and the same: she went to Bowness High School, and her childhood was filled with memories of Bowness Park. She left Montgomery as a young woman twenty years ago; now a resident of Silver Springs, just north across the river from Bowness, she often went jogging through Bowmont

Park, across Bowness Bridge and along Bow Crescent.

Now the neighbourhood that still felt like home to her was in distress. For her first two days of volunteering, Monica stayed until around eight o'clock and returned at eight the following morning. She was a manager at a charter airline, but she told her employer she wouldn't be in for several days; that didn't go over well, but she didn't care. This was something she needed to do.

Brittney had come down to volunteer in Bowness with her company. She had been volunteering for a few days now and had found a rhythm in her work. Wednesday was Monica's third day volunteering, and she met Brittney on Bow Crescent. There was an instant connection between the two outgoing, bubbly personalities, and they soon found themselves working together to try and organize the somewhat scattered volunteer effort.

Groups and individuals were coming out in droves, but there was no higher direction, no method for steering the effort. The two women began pointing volunteers toward homes that required help, making sure that everyone who needed workers would get them.

Monica had done everything she could to rally people to come out, and the street was humming with activity. The summer thundershowers from the previous day had given way to warm and sunny weather. Coupled with the hard, draining work, volunteers found themselves easily tiring out in the hot sun.

While Brittney said farewell to her work companions in

the early evening, Monica found a wooden bench and put it in front of Ritch and Cathy's home, where a small food station had been set up by some volunteers. Placed under their lilac bushes, the bench provided a pleasant spot to rest, and Monica was pleased with the idea. Sitting on the bench, she found herself staring at the small empty lot directly across the street. The pavement in front of it had been washed away and a large pool of water had collected, but the lot itself was lush and green, with only a blue tented carport and a small house on the property.

Brittney came by and found Monica, and the two of them began talking about the empty lot. Ideas began pouring out of them, building upon each other's suggestions one after another.

That would be a nice spot in the shade for people to rest.

We could have food there.

And cold drinks!

Maybe a bar, we could serve beer!

There's enough tables and chairs in the rubbish that we could use...

... and decorate it! Maybe get donations!

They began scouring the street and rubbish piles for whatever they could salvage, setting them up on the lot, creating a makeshift bar and food area inside the blue tent. They assumed the land was abandoned, as it surely seemed to be. There was an unstable plank of wood over the water, but a more reliable crossing was soon built. Some discarded antlers were added to the decor.

Monica said she wasn't able to come down the next day, but Brittney said she could come in the afternoon and try to fix things up a bit more if Monica could organize the beer and other donations. (Monica had become friendly with the police officers patrolling the area; when she asked whether she'd need to get a liquor license for distributing cold beer to the people working, the cops suggested they'd look the other way so long as things didn't get out of hand.)

Before leaving, the two women made a sign advertising the grand opening the following day. They called it the Moat.

AT HALF PAST THREE THURSDAY MORNING, a Canadian Pacific Railway train with more than one hundred cars began crossing the Bonnybrook Bridge over the swollen Bow River southeast of the city centre. The bridge, constructed in 1912, was unique in the city in that it was not built into the bedrock. The floodwaters of the past week had caused scouring under one of the bridge piers, resulting in instability. Once the majority of the train had crossed, the bridge could take no more and gave way.

Six cars remained on the partially collapsed bridge, five of them filled with liquid petroleum products, hanging precariously over the Bow as the bridge threatened to fall entirely. The crisis would feature sharp banter in the media between Nenshi and Hunter Harrison, the CEO of Canadian Pacific.

The mayor wondered aloud to reporters whether the recent deep cuts at the railway had included firing bridge inspectors; he wondered why municipalities were powerless to regulate railways, yet it was city crews putting their lives in jeopardy to resolve the situation.

CP issued a statement claiming the bridge had been inspected Saturday and the tracks on Monday. Harrison would later claim the bridge was inspected five times since the flood. Engineers for the company would tell the media the bridge was inspected eighteen times since the flood. Divers, though, were not deployed as it was considered too dangerous given current river levels. Suspending usage of the bridge in the meantime was deemed unnecessary.

The incident would spark a larger debate about the responsibilities and oversight of the rail industry. But more immediately, it would strain an already stretched emergency force in a city still reeling from a major disaster. The area was evacuated, including the city sewage treatment plant, and Deerfoot Trail was shut down as a precaution as engineers worked to pump the chemicals out of the cars before attempting to move them.

STEVE'S FRIENDS HAD BEEN USING their audio/visual company to stock and distribute generators and pumps during the recovery. Social media acted as a simple way to get the word out across the city: We've got pumps, who needs them? The reply came that a pump was needed at the Roxboro Community Centre, and Steve and his roommate Donovan headed down there.

They found several volunteers cleaning out the basement when they arrived. Hey, we're here with a pump! Oh, great!

There was a moment of awkwardness: Steve and Donovan thought they were just dropping off the pump and leaving; the volunteers thought it would be set up for them. None of them had ever used a pump before.

Steve and Donovan agreed to set it up, figuring out the mechanics of the machine while the volunteers continued clearing out things from the basement.

Once the pump was operational, the volunteers said they were leaving. Again, miscommunication was apparent: they believed Steve and Donovan were intending to relieve them of their work and monitor the pump.

Though the situation was not what they expected, the two roommates were game to help, and they spent the next six hours cleaning out the community centre basement together. There was a crawlspace filled with party supplies, mattress, and things ruined beyond recognition. The floor was again slippery and muddy, and the lifting was hard on Steve's knee. Meanwhile, there was a sharp learning curve with the pump, which kept clogging with mud.

By the evening, Steve's knee was in terrible shape, and as they headed home, he knew he wouldn't be volunteering the next day.

Instead, Steve spent Friday at home on his computer. By this point, Steve had become known as a key distributor of recovery information, particularly for people looking for where to volunteer. Now with his full focus dedicated to social media, he did what he could to make sure people were connected with the information they needed to be effective.

The mechanics of it were simple enough: Steve posted something online, perhaps an address that needed help; being a serial organizer by trade, he had many online friends who were themselves important nodes on social networks; these people re-posted his calls for help, thus spreading the original post to thousands of Calgarians in just minutes. Silly videos go viral on a weekly basis. This was the same principle, but on a local level and for the purposes of harnessing the otherwise largely directionless volunteer machine.

MONICA SPENT MUCH OF THURSDAY at home, trying to organize donations for the Moat. She envisioned it as a social hub for the neighbourhood, a way to take care of both the people who had been hit by the flood and the people who were taking care of them.

Brittney came back to Bow Crescent around two o'clock Thursday afternoon, but found that someone had trespassed on their lot: there was food inside the tent—apparently to keep it out of the sun—and their carefully arranged salvaged furniture had been moved. Brittney spent the next few hours reorganizing the Moat and getting it ready.

In fact, the lot was not abandoned. It was owned by Kim, who lived across the street with his wife, and the small house on the lot had been lived in by his son prior to the flood. Kim had invited some volunteers with a food station to move their goods into the tent so as to keep them out of the sun, unaware of what Monica and Brittney were planning on his land.

Monica had arranged for donated beer from a craft brewery, and a delivery trailer arrived around four o'clock. The beer was set out on a table with ice to chill it. Volunteers, seeing the endeavour, brought snacks and sandwiches over to contribute. By the time Monica herself arrived, there were already more than twenty people in the makeshift volunteer bar. The Moat was a success.

Pieces of Bristol board were taped up on the beer company's trailer, each with different headings: What made you cry? What is your favorite moment? What made you smile today? Markers were provided for people to share their memories and thank those who had helped them, whether their names were known or not.

Brittney soon had to leave for a soccer game. Since she would shortly be leaving town for ten days, this was her final moment to enjoy what they had created. The two women thanked each other and hugged, and that was it. The Moat was now Monica's to sustain.

Dan and Meera had come for one final day of volunteering

on Bow Crescent. They had spent a few hours helping Ritch and Cathy clear out their yard. As they were leaving, they saw the gathering of people across the street at the Moat. Let's go check it out, said Dan, I could really use a beer right now.

They first thought it must be someone's private residence, but it quickly became apparent that it was a community gathering. Despite the free alcohol, no one seemed to be drunk or causing trouble. It was a fun and friendly atmosphere.

A cop drove up to the Moat on an ATV. Dan quickly looked around and realized there was almost certainly no liquor license for this makeshift bar where dozens of people were drinking openly. Hey! yelled the cop, and the beer in Dan's hand felt heavy all of a sudden. Hey! Does anyone have any bolt cutters?

Dan and Meera left after a quick drink and a snack. The party at the Moat continued until around dusk, when Monica began shutting it down and everyone went home.

FIVE DAYS AFTER SHE WAS FIRST called to set up the evacuation centre, Louise was sent home by Tom. She was burned out from the long shifts, at least sixteen hours each day. The emotional toll had also hit her hard. Seeing the hundreds of people despairing, listening to their stories as they wept, all while trying to create order in a chaotic, fast-changing situation—all of this had left her hollow.

But she kept it to herself for the most part. After a three-day rest, she was back at work Friday. Many people had by now left the evacuation centre to camp or stay with family and friends, both on and off the reserve. A few had gone to hotels in towns or cities.

But nearly all of the displaced residents wanted above all else to go home. Even if they weren't yet allowed to begin the clean-up and recovery, they wanted to see the damage. Their minds could only image what the river had done to their homes. The powerful images and videos had shocked them as they had everyone else. They understood that it would be bad. But until they had a visual, until they saw the reality, their imaginations would torture them.

The tradition of governance in Blackfoot culture is such that people regularly take their concerns, opinions and requests directly to their leaders. Tom, along with the chief and council, were inundated through the week with calls asking for permission to return home.

Arrangements were made to escort displaced residents who wished to see their homes. One day was allotted for each community. Before departing from the sportsplex, everyone was given rubber boots, which were to be discarded after their visit. Gloves and masks were distributed. Rules were given: only five minutes inside the house, no touching or taking anything. Their homes were covered with the filth and sewage of a major city. The health risks were significant.

School buses drove them down into the flooded territory. The trip to the communities on the south side of the river took much longer because the bridge was out.

For three days, Louise went along with the residents of North Camp, South Camp, and North Chicago. Together with a Red Cross worker, she would be charged with escorting each of the families back inside their homes, one home at a time. Louise had spoken to some of the Red Cross workers who had seen the devastation first-hand. They warned her what it would be like. But there was no preparing for it.

There was a great amount of loss: more than two hundred homes were damaged, many beyond repair. Several had been lifted from their foundation by the river and crashed into other houses. The stench was horrible.

The reaction of the residents varied, but the emotions were always strong. Some cried loudly. Others were silent. A few broke down completely. Grown men wept openly. These were people at their most raw. After five minutes they had to leave the house and Louise continued to the next one.

THE MOAT CONTINUED FRIDAY and over the weekend, with Monica the driving force behind it. In just a few short days, it had become a fully-accepted institution, organically filling a need among the volunteers and victims.

On Friday, Kim came over to see what had become of his

supposedly abandoned lot.   Someone introduced him to Monica, who was stunned to hear that the man she was shaking hands with owned the land her volunteer bar was squatting on. Well, what do you think?

I love it! I'm just happy someone did something positive with it. This is great.

The food and beverage donations continued from local businesses, especially a Bownesian pizzeria and an Alberta craft brewery. The police did indeed look the other way on the open liquor; no problematic issues arose and the atmosphere was positive. The Moat didn't start serving beer until five o'clock each day. Some people stopped by for a quick break around that time, others continued working and came later when their day was finished.

It lifted the spirits of both Bownesians and volunteers who were struggling with the clean-up effort, which had now progressed quite a bit in just a week. Now, with the end of the month upon them and Canada Day approaching, it was time for something special.

Monica wanted to transform the casual atmosphere of the Moat, which averaged up to one hundred people ordinarily, into a celebration of the post-flood atmosphere. She arranged for enough food and drink for hundreds of people (though with less alcohol, as the party would start earlier in the day) as well as a face painter, DJ and balloons. She made sure everyone knew something big was happening at the Moat.

There was more to the plan, but Monica wouldn't reveal

it. There was a surprise, but she wouldn't say what. Around the appointed hour of seven o'clock, some people began leaving to go back to home, or to continue working on their flooded houses. Monica pleaded with them to stay a little while longer. No one knew why. They hadn't noticed the plainclothes security men who had joined the party.

Soon, walking down the street, shaking hands and flashing his million-watt grin, came Nenshi. He received a hero's welcome from the Moat, glad-handing through the crowd, posing for photographs, completely in his element.

Up until that point, the Moat had seemed special only within that small Bownesian world, something like a group of neighbourhood kids setting up a popular lemonade stand. But the surprise appearance of Nenshi, who had become for the city both the representation of hope and an omnipresent celebrity, gave it larger significance. This was just one community gathering on one street in one neighbourhood among the widespread devastation; but it was worth a personal visit from the mayor, and after all that had happened, it did feel special.

Nenshi stood on the picnic table and addressed the crowd, signed the Moat banner, took photos and chatted with residents. If anyone had a complaint with the City or the mayor himself, no one raised it. It wasn't the moment. After forty minutes, the jovial man and his entourage continued on down the street.

The party continued for a few more hours, ending once again around dusk. Canada Day marked the end of the

Moat. Monica would come visit her newfound friends on Bow Crescent when she could. But she also had to get back to her regular life, to her job, to her son. Most of the homes were now at or near the point where volunteer labour would need to be replaced with contractors and tradespeople. Anyone can tear out soggy drywall, but most people need an electrician to rewire a house.

Bowness was not yet healed, but now it would be increasingly left to convalesce on its own, without the legions of volunteers, without the Moat. Ordinary life had begun to creep back into the city: the streets were generally clear and repaired, downtown was open again, and the public's focus had shifted towards High River, which was just reopening, along with the questionable status of the upcoming Stampede.

The Moat had both represented and facilitated the post-flood outpouring of neighbourly support and community strength, and had imbued victims with a sense of optimism in the face of often total loss. Now things would be different. Now they had to move forward more or less on their own as the volunteers began returning to their normal lives.

WITH THE BRIEF VISITS TO their ruined homes granted, the next step was to start a process for getting Siksika residents back to their houses to begin the clean-up process. Tom had been told by the province that their Rapid Assessment

Structural Team was available. The team was mobilized to quickly evaluate buildings and infrastructure after disasters, such as the Slave Lake fire that destroyed that town in 2011. Tom requested them immediately, and the team assessed two hundred fifty homes in less than three days, clearing the primary hurdle to starting the clean-up. Several dozen families were allowed to return home soon after. Tom ordered dumpsters to be placed in clean-up areas for the rubbish, as well as large shipping containers for people to store undamaged or salvaged items with their own padlocks.

Volunteers, particularly through charity groups such as Red Cross and Samaritan's Purse, came to assist with the length and difficult process of recovery. But Louise had her own recovery to deal with. Not long after her experience with residents re-entering their homes, Louise began a vacation leave that had been scheduled prior to the disaster.

The time off was hardly relaxing. She couldn't sleep at night. Her headaches increased in frequency and severity. She began seeing a doctor, who diagnosed her symptoms as post-traumatic stress disorder. A spiral into depression followed.

Louise was put on medical leave after her vacation time ended. She suffered flashbacks of the people she had helped: how they cried, how broken they were. She had accumulated their collective anguish, and it had broken her, too.

After the terrible shock of seeing video of their unexpectedly flooded High River house, Jeremy and Lani endured an emotional rollercoaster ride: frustration at the missing or misleading information being reported; helplessness at being unable to return home; anger at the authorities for their handling of the situation; confusion about the timeline for return, which changed from three weeks, to three-to-five weeks, to five-to-seven weeks, back to three weeks. They followed the news carefully, but derived little clarity or reassurance.

There was word that the northwest section of the town would selectively open the following day, only for residents and their contractors. Most of High River, including Jeremy and Lani's house on the east side of town, remained under a stringent blockade.

With nothing to do, no access to his own house, going stir-crazy with his family and Lani's mother and sister under one roof, Jeremy decided to go back to High River.

With his brother's RV, Jeremy arrived early in the afternoon on June 30, ten days since the flood first hit. He parked at a landscaping business on the north side of the town, which Jeremy's employer had been utilizing as a temporary yard since the flood. Across the road were the rodeo grounds, where entry passes were being handed out to residents and their contractors. Access to the town was strictly controlled, and police were checking everyone for passes.

Jeremy needed to find an in. The owner of the landscaping business offered to lend him a flat deck truck to get around town. Jeremy's boss had left a dump trailer there, and he attached it to the truck and drove to the rodeo grounds.

He parked the truck and began approaching residents, explaining who he was, that he wanted to help, trying to convince someone to register him as their contractor so he could get a pass. But these were distraught, emotional, shell-shocked people: residents who, like Jeremy, were forced suddenly from their homes, starved of information for weeks, confused and concerned about their property and belongings. Their minds were elsewhere; Jeremy's pleas didn't even register.

After several attempts, he repeated his request to someone and saw the glaze disappear from their eyes. Yeah, said the man, come with me. Jeremy got his pass, then drove the truck to the checkpoint. He showed the pass and was waved through. He was now free to drive anywhere he liked within the reopened northwest.

The devastation was everywhere and overwhelming. Random garbage was strewn everywhere. Yards and gardens had disappeared, with most plant life unable to survive the toxic flood waters and residue. Water lines marked houses with eerie reminders: one foot, two feet, one metre, two metres. Absolutely everything was covered with sewage-contaminated silt, and a horrible stench burned the nostrils and turned the stomach. The streets were crowded with people and vehicles. Some residents walked around with deadened expressions; others wept openly. It seemed everyone was in shock, unable to process the loss.

Jeremy tried not to think of his own house on the other side of town. He made himself busy, hauling away the piles of ruined and stinking garbage that were once people's possessions, which collected on the sides of the roads as residents began the daunting task of cleaning up.

The work was draining, and not only for the homeowners. It was difficult not to be affected by the scene, by the loss. The reopened areas were primarily around the golf course, populated with large, expensive homes belonging to comparatively well-off families. But even if the flood was not financially crippling to them—and it was for some, to be sure—every family of any social standing has irreplaceables, treasures bought not with money but with memories. Something in human nature compels us to collect such things; and, in suburban Canadian homes, they are often stored in the basement for safekeeping: photo albums, letters, diaries, heirlooms, childhood keepsakes, marriage certificates. These were the items unceremoniously hauled up from basements and dumped, stinking and wet, onto the sidewalk for Jeremy to haul away to the dump. No amount of money in the world could replace these things.

The mood was sour, and interactions were often strained. People were tired and depressed, and there was a broad underlying feeling of anger or resentment towards various levels of government for their handling of the situation. It was hard, especially in the first few days, for people who had suffered such personal hardship and loss to look at things from any viewpoint but their own. Community solidarity would come soon, but for the first day or two, Jeremy sensed frustration about to boil over everywhere.

There was no food, no restaurants, no grocery stores. Some people were passing out muffins and fruit and other things they had brought, but Jeremy couldn't eat. The food he was given, he gave away. It wasn't until eight or nine o'clock at night, when he returned to the RV, that he bothered to eat. The motor home was hardly luxurious—an older, smaller vehicle—but it was home for now. Cell phone reception had not yet been restored, so he was cut off from his family. All he had were the canned soups, frozen burgers, and cold beers stocked his brother.

Jeremy spent the next two days doing much of the same work. At the end of each day he would wipe his muddy boots on a patch of grass; the grass, poisoned by the biohaz-ardous mud, quickly died. Each day he would respond to the thanks of residents by reminding them that his part of town would be open eventually. Don't forget about us. We'll need help, too.

After three days of volunteering, Jeremy was burnt out and went back to his family in Calgary.

On July 2, Florence's family returned to her home in High River. Her daughter Pat and her husband Laine came up from their home in Crowsnest Pass, along with Alanna and her husband Jon. Alanna had come the previous day for a brief visit with her mother, step-father and Ken, but everyone else was seeing the effects of the flood for the first time.

There were incredible sights on the drive into the town. The mud and debris was everywhere. The railway tracks were bent and twisted like a roller-coaster. It seemed every house and business on every street was affected, many of them catastrophically. The sounds of generators and heavy machinery filled the hot, humid air. Each house had a pile of rubbish in front of it as work crews hauled things out into the street.

Florence's house was designated as 'red', the worst of the four colour codes. Red indicated the home was unfit for habitation, for any number of possible reasons. But after waiting so long, they were hardly going to be satisfied with an outside view of the family home, and the group went inside.

The water had not reached the main floor. The weather was very hot and humid, which made the smell inside that much worse. The lack of ventilation combined with many days of heat had turned the house into a perfect incubator for mould, which was the overwhelming odour inside.

They gathered a few things from the main floor to take out, mostly old family photographs and other keepsakes. Then they ventured downstairs.

The basement was destroyed. Everything was muddy and thrown about. Few things were readily identifiable beyond the large pieces of furniture. The basement refrigerator had been left without power for nearly two weeks, and the rotten food inside produced a powerful stench. They hauled it up and out of the house—a disgusting job—and deposited it on the front lawn to be taken away.

That was all that could be done that first day. Between the shock of seeing the house, the size of the cleanup task, and the repulsive smell, they decided they weren't prepared to do much more that day.

Laine and Pat were staying with family in north Calgary, about an hour's commute from High River in good traffic. They both happened to be on vacation leave from work at that time, so they were the most available to work on the house. They returned to High River the next day and got started, working in the yard and the garage. Each day they would return, working about fourteen hours before making the drive back into Calgary. Other family members would pitch in when they could.

The first volunteers to join them were a corporate group from the head offices of a financial organization. There were ten of them, and they focused on cleaning out the garage. The house was structurally unstable with the collapsed basement wall. Before the real work in the basement could begin, the house needed to be professionally assessed and the main beams shored up with temporary supports. Structural engineers were in high demand, and there were none available for the time being, so Florence's house sat broken and dirty while the work continued around it.

FOLLOWING HIS THREE DAYS of volunteering, Jeremy needed a change of pace. The emotional toll exacted by the devastation, coupled with his own stress and worry, was grinding him down. He returned to his regular construction job, working to build fences on acreages outside the town, staying overnight in the RV at the landscape company.

He did two days of this work. On the second day, he got word from Lani that their neighbourhood was reopening. There had been talk and rumours for a few days already, but they had little reason to hope. Their timeline had jumped all over the place, anywhere from days to weeks. Now it was really happening. It was July 4, exactly two weeks after they had been evacuated.

Jeremy drove back to Calgary and picked Lani up around four o'clock. They drove south back to High River and headed for the rodeo grounds to register and receive their homeowners' package. They were told their home was classified 'red'. This did not surprise them, having seen video and images of their house underwater. The package was very generic and basic, mostly hand-out information on what to do post-flood and precautions to take during clean-up.

Well, how do we get to our house? The official who had given them the package looked confused. What do you mean? You just drive there.

Not long before that day, the official timeline had indicated weeks—two, three, maybe more—would be the waiting period for reentry. The reasons given usually related to safety and health concerns. There had been a great deal of public pressure for officials to open the town sooner, but they had refused. For all Jeremy and Lani knew, the water had yet to fully subside.

But the streets were dry as they drove to their house. The heavy roadblocks Jeremy had seen while working in the northwest were gone. There were no pass checks, no guards. The town was open, and they were free to go home. It was infuriating; there seemed to be no obvious reason to have kept residents out this long. How much sooner could we have been here?

But there would be time for anger later. Right now, the house was the priority.

Jeremy asked his wife: Are you prepared for this? Yes, she said. I know how bad it's going to be. What I'm looking for... is one thing. I don't know which thing, but... something I didn't expect to survive that survived. If I can find that one thing, I'll be all right.

Their corner lot was visible from a distance: the wooden fence was lying flat and broken, the posts having been lifted out of the ground; a boat trailer they'd never seen before was sitting on the fence; reeds and grass from the fields surrounding the town were everywhere. They parked and walked up to the house and saw the water line, an eerie and frightening reminder that this spot was a lake not two weeks earlier.

Inside, the house was unrecognizable. The water had reached the main floor; the water mark showed there had been about a foot of water on this level. The hardwood floors had expanded and buckled nearly everywhere in the house, flipping over much of the furniture; the floor in the master bedroom looked like a roller-coaster track. In the kitchen, the dishes from the barbecued chicken supper they'd shared with their friends before the evacuation still sat on the counter.

Jeremy and Lani ventured down to the basement. The stench was potent on the main floor, but here it became overwhelming. The floor was thick with sludge, largely a mix of dirt and sewage. The basement was very dark, and it was difficult to see clearly. One of the windows had broken and the glass had been scattered by the water. Part of the ceiling had collapsed.

When the 340,000 litres of water that had filled the modest basement began to leave through the floor drain in the laundry room, it created a current inside the house that pulled things along with it. The result was a soggy, stinking pile that blocked access to the laundry room door. Lani examined the pile: it was taller than her, and though it was surely made of their belongings, she could not identify them.

The pillows, blankets and upholstery, which had retained water the longest, were covered with white mould. Some of the walls had black mould. The job before them was overwhelming to the point of being incomprehensible.

But the experience itself—walking through the house, seeing the damage, smelling the smells—was not devastating, certainly not compared to seeing that video online. Then, they had not been braced for anything close to the reality; after that video, they had set aside all hope for their home, and that made the reentry more of a clinical excercise, almost cathartic after all the frustration and waiting.

And Lani had found her one thing: the photo album from their wedding, which Jeremy had brought upstairs and set on top of a box before they left. The bottom of the box was soggy, but the photo album was untouched. Lani held it tightly as they left their home once again and drove back to Calgary.

THE MORNING AFTER JEREMY and Lani reentered their house, Jeremy's brother took the bus down from Edmonton, and he and Jeremy drove to High River in the RV. Lani stayed home to watch the girls.

They stopped to get supplies before leaving the city: buckets, gloves, masks. When they arrived at the house, they assessed the task before them, and their day began with a feeling not unlike defeat. What do we do? Where do we start? Everything was ruined and everything was filthy.

The logical starting point was the basement. The laundry room and bathroom were both blocked by large piles of rubbish. They began grabbing things from the piles and carrying them up and out, dumping them in a new pile outside. Soon they realized it was much smarter to fill bins with shovels and then dump the bins outside. Neither man had coveralls, only boots and jeans and T-shirts, and they were soon covered in putrid sediment.

The work was tiring. Though the masks provided a level of health protection against the biohazardous muck, it did nothing for the smell, which filled their mouths and noses as they breathed heavily with exercise. Jeremy's brother did not have a weak stomach, but the stench nauseated him to the point of vomiting.

The piles gradually diminished, and they were able to enter the laundry room and open the window to begin ventilating the basement. But the bathroom door wouldn't budge: a cabinet inside had fallen against it, and the wooden door was swollen shut against the frame. Jeremy kicked in the door and shoved the cabinet aside to enter the bathroom. But the window also refused to open, stuck shut from sediment. He tried opening it from outside the house, but wound up breaking the glass in the process.

Well, there's one more thing to fix, he thought as he kicked in the rest of the window.

Having cleared out the piles, opened the rooms and begun ventilating the basement was enough work for one day. Jeremy and his brother ate and slept in the motor home that night, rising early the next morning to begin again.

They weren't alone on the second day. Lani came down with family and a few friends to pitch in. But what was most remarkable were the people they didn't know.

The volunteers began arriving first thing in the morning. By the afternoon, Jeremy counted twenty-six people in the house, most of whom were complete strangers. They were tearing out soaked drywall and hauling out ruined belongings. Massive piles began growing outside.

Jeremy and Lani were amazed. The job that had seemed enormous and complex was advancing at lightning pace. Their house was being completely gutted, and the sooner the better.

The work was not only physically tiring but emotionally draining. Even the people who had never met the owners before and had no connection to them were visibly affected by the total loss of everything, by the bits of people's lives scattered in the waste, by the children's toys strewn about carelessly by the flood waters.

Neither parent could bring themselves to perform the heart-wrenching chore of cleaning out their little girls' playroom in the basement. The thought sickened them, and they left it to others to throw out their ruined toys and childhood treasures.

When Lani had first arrived at the house that day, the

work was well underway and the piles outside were sizeable. As the cleanup progressed, the piles grew larger, and the sight of them affected her more than she expected. Their belongings, the physical representations of their lives, were being unceremoniously chucked into stinking heaps by complete strangers. She knew, of course, that it had to happen. But when those piles of ruins were inside the house, they still had stuff; now they had nothing.

At one point, a motorcycle roared up the street and pulled up onto the remnants of their lawn. Jeremy watched the rider dismount: though she was about fifty, she was surely over six feet tall and looked hard as nails. So, where do I help?

Are you real? thought Jeremy. But he said: Well, you can pick that house, or that house, or our house. Everyone needs help. The woman went inside. She smelled and saw the destruction, watched the people working. Like many others, she was stunned and overwhelmed, and it was some time before she began working.

The basement was essentially gutted by the end of the day. The piles of discarded drywall and other rubbish were taller than the railing on the deck, taller than a man. There were no dumpsters.

When Jeremy and Lani came back the following morning, they were amazed to see many of the same faces from the day before. The work began again, and the main floor was ripped apart. Lani spent much of the day applying for funding under the province's Disaster Recovery Program.

A family came down to volunteer, a father with his sons

and daughter. The daughter was in her mid-twenties and quite attractive. Despite the dirtiness of the job, she wore tiny shorts and a tank top, with her hair, make-up and nails fully done. She was a comical contrast to the legions of volunteers equipped from head-to-toe in coveralls and masks. Jeremy caught sight of her a couple of hours later as she hauled rubbish out of the house, completely caked in mud.

By the end of the day, all that could be done had been done. In a mere three days, the house had been stripped of all its losses, from drywall to furniture to treasured keep-sakes. It would remain in that broken state for a long time. Jeremy and Lani thanked their volunteers, closed the door, and drove back to Calgary, unsure of what would be next.

LAINE AND PAT CONTINUED WORKING to clean the garage and the yard, but there was only so much to be done in these areas. The main job still lay inside the house Pat's father had built, which was structurally unstable and in need of assessment.

After a week and a half of clean-up, a volunteer who had been working in the neighbour's yard offered to help. He was an architect and he worked with a structural engineer. Pat and Laine, along with the rest of the family, were wary of spending a great deal of money on clean-up and repair costs, as no one was sure whether the house could be saved at all. But the men offered their services at no charge, an unexpected moment of generosity that touched the family deeply.

Once assessed, the house needed temporary metal tele-posts to support the structure. Laine and a friend installed them according to the engineer's specifications. Once the house was made stable, they knocked out more bricks in the punctured basement wall to facilitate the clean-up process, which they began in earnest.

While cleaning, they came across a strange item sitting amidst the rubbish in the basement. It was round, almost plump, like an oversized football. They couldn't figure out for the life of them what it was. After a comically lengthy investigation, they determined it to be a once-frozen plastic-wrapped turkey that had floated over from the upturned freezer. It provided a much-needed lighthearted moment, and the men laughed harder than they likely would have had they not been surrounded by so much sadness.

Pat and Laine went back to their home in Crowsnest Pass occasionally, but mostly they stayed in Calgary and contin-ued working on the house. The basement clean-up progressed with the help of volunteers, though some of them did not feel comfortable entering the beaten-down house for fear of its collapse.

Lyle had been a hunter who reloaded shells as a hobby. When he died, all of his ammunition and gunpowder remained in a cabinet in the basement, undisturbed until the flood. The water knocked over the cabinet, carrying bullets, casings and primers everywhere. In a small town with a fairly rural culture, this was a common issue after the flood, and the RCMP organized a drive to have people bring in their flooded guns and ammunition for safe disposal. As Pat drove a truckload of her father's wet gunpower, shells and bullets to the RCMP office, she feared she'd be arrested for possessing so much ammunition. But they accepted her story; they'd likely heard stranger ones before.

Even with the hole in the wall providing easy access, the basement clean-up was a nightmare. The heat and smell only added to the discomfort of the job. There was about four feet of sludge at the bottom, mostly mud and silt with a smell of sewage and gasoline. Though the bulk of the ammunition had been removed, there were still live rounds mixed into the rubbish, and caution had to be used, particularly with shovels and metal tools.

When soaked with water, everything increases in weight. Fibreglass insulation, normally light, feels like carrying bags of sand, and the old horsehair-stuffed couch in the basement had gained hundreds of pounds.

The upright piano that Lyle had bought and lovingly restored for his young wife was completely ruined. Florence and her daughters and grandchildren had played it throughout the decades, filling the house with music, and it was as treasured and irreplaceable as an old family photo album. But now it was hacked apart into more manageable pieces and taken out of the house the way Lyle had brought it in: through a hole in the basement wall.

EPILOGUE

The Alberta government estimated the area directly impacted by floodwater to be 55,000 km², roughly equivalent to the size of Nova Scotia. Fourteen thousand five hundred homes were damaged. Thirty provincial roads and highways were closed or damaged. Two hundred bridges required varying degrees of repair, from minor fixes to complete replacement. Many apartment buildings, condominiums, and commercial high-rises required a great deal of repair to their operational infrastructure, much of it located in basements. Elevators, boilers, furnaces, generators all needed fixing or replacing. Contractors, tradespeople and engineers were booked solid for weeks and months afterwards.

The provincial government estimated the total cost to be more than $6 billion. The insurable costs of the disaster were estimated to be more than $1.7 billion. It ranked as the costliest disaster in Canadian history, ahead of the 1998 Ice Storm in the central and eastern provinces, which had insurable losses of $1.6 billion and total costs of about $3 billion.

On Monday, June 24, four days after the flood hit, the president of the Calgary Stampede announced that the show would go on "come hell or high water," a phrase that likely has its origins in cattle ranching in the western United States around the turn of the 20th century. Cowboys driving their stock to the railway for shipment had to make their destination on schedule. They couldn't afford to let rivers nor difficult terrain slow them down.

The idiom had begun appearing on social media sometime before the Monday announcement, a fitting reference to the tenacity of Albertans in the face of a disaster. It's unclear whether it was first attached in reference to the Stampede as a deliberate marketing move or as an innocent comment, but it soon took off as the slogan for the 2014 edition of the event, with advertising and memorabilia featuring it prominently.

The flat grounds alongside the Elbow River had been hit hard. Aside from the clean-up and terraforming needed, a great deal of infrastructure needed to be replaced or repaired. Millions of dollars went into these repairs, and hundreds of volunteers responded to accomplish what many thought impossible. Though the Saddledome would not be ready in time and major concerts would be cancelled, the event otherwise opened as scheduled. Media across the country devoted more attention than usual to the opening of the world's richest rodeo and accompanying festival, praising the dogged hard work of Albertans.

Though the event raised $2.1 million for the Red Cross through T-shirt sales, many were critical of the money and volunteers put towards salvaging a private business endeavour when there was still a great deal of suffering, particularly in High River and Siksika. Others pointed out that the Stampede draws an enormous amount of tourism dollars into the city and province; the total attendance figure of 1.1 million for 2013 was down a few hundred thousand from 2012's all-time record, but on par with years previous. In 2009, Stampede officials estimated the gross economic benefit of the ten-day event for the city to be $172 million, and $226 million for Alberta; these numbers place it ahead of all other festivals in the country.

Economics aside, it was also argued that the Stampede was an important emblem of Calgary's cultural heritage; it is worth noting, however, that it originated with an American who had tried to pitch the idea to several other cities, and indeed held it elsewhere for several years after the first 1912 event when his Calgary partners refused to pay for another.

The majority of Calgarians and Albertans, though, were proud to see the Stampede back on its feet against long odds, standing as a symbol of southern Alberta's potential for recovery. Chris Hadfield, the celebrated Canadian astronaut recently returned from the International Space Station, was a universally popular choice for parade marshal. The event featured various tributes to the victims and volunteers, and the general spirit was one of celebration, of Alberta and Calgary back on their feet to greet the world.

A benefit concert was organized for August, with big-name Canadian musicians and bands performing at McMahon Stadium. Over 30,000 people attended, including the prime minister and premier, and the event was nationally televised. More than $1.5 million was raised for flood relief.

The Calgary Zoo suffered significant and costly damage to many buildings and infrastructure, estimated at $50 million. Some buildings, depending on their location and construction, took on only a few centimetres of water; others saw several metres. The ageing South America building was condemned, and the animals it housed were permanently sent to other zoos. In addition to the vast clean-up and repairs, significant effort was directed towards post-flood animal care, particularly for those animals who stayed behind.

There was significant public support for the zoo in the weeks and months after the flood. Donation drives and fundraising ventures were organized to help fund the rebuild of the zoo, and cover the operating losses due to the lengthy closure. It wasn't until late November—five months after the flood—that the zoo was able to fully open again.

Having gone many decades and generations without a flood of the severity that marked those in the late 19th century and early 20th century, many people, particularly in Calgary, had either forgotten or never known that the area was prone to flooding. It was a natural creep of confidence over a long span of time: after early Calgary was devastated by major floods, many chose not to rebuild on the flat low riverbanks, seeking higher ground. But as the years went by without a significant flood event, the city continued to grow. Memories of the risk faded, and the land was redeveloped. Dams were built upstream to mitigate and manage seasonal flooding, increasing the sense of security. After enough years, the people deciding where to build houses or office buildings had no personal memory of the great floods of a bygone era.

When the Drop-In Centre building was constructed in the East Village very near the river, precautions were taken. Much of the important equipment and operational infrastructure that would normally be housed in the basement—heaters, generators, boilers, electrical panels—was installed on the seventh floor. The floodwater filled the DI's basement and the laundry facilities were lost, a significant expense. But once the building was cleaned by legions of volunteers and minor repairs performed, it was allowed to re-open in a matter of days, not weeks or months.

In one sense, the situation echoes the old warning that those who do not take heed of history are doomed to repeat it. But the city can hardly be moved now. Relocating smaller towns like High River and Canmore would be logistical, political and economical nightmares; the idea of reshaping the heart of a major metropolitan centre like Calgary—with its countless billions of dollars of skyscrapers and infrastructure and parks and freeways—is a non-starter. The flood raised awareness of the problem to the point of forcing the issue, but no one can unbuild a city.

In November 2013, the Alberta government announced a commitment to flood mitigation projects on the Highwood, Elbow and Bow rivers, among others. Studies were launched to examine proposals, such as a diversion channel around High River, and a dry dam on the Elbow upstream of the city. The City of Calgary also began studying the idea of an underground flood diversion from the Glenmore Reservoir to the Bow River, slicing a long stretch beneath the city.

The political fallout from the flood was substantial, much of it centering on High River: the sealing off of the town; the lengthy delay in allowing residents to return; the search of evacuated homes for weapons by the RCMP; a statement by a government-hired engineer, caught secretly on video, admitting that officials sacrificed a neighbourhood that likely would not have flooded in an attempt to save other parts of the town (the province quickly denied this); a plan by the town to undevelop a flood-prone neighbourhood, unilaterally if necessary, and return it to its natural state.

There was also great criticism of the province's handling of the situation both before and after the waters came. How could they not know? Why was there no warning?

An investigation by *Calgary Herald* reporters found several questionable decisions made by provincial forecasters in the days leading up to the flood. Particularly damning were suggestions by officials that the astounding river data readings in the hours prior to the flood were distrusted by forecasters because they seemed impossibly high. The province ordered a review of the river forecast section's handling of the disaster.

The province also found itself in a controversy over its mapping of areas at risk of flooding. The government announced four categories of land near flood-prone rivers: floodway, flood fringe, overland flow, and areas under review. The floodways are areas most expected to flood, and Premier Redford had offered to buy the homes of residents in these areas at the previously assessed value. But when the maps were released to the public, High River residents found most of their houses were considered flood fringe, excluding them from buyouts and requiring them to flood-proof their homes in order to be eligible for provincial relief funding after future disasters. The Alberta government offered full buyouts for 254 floodway homes in the province; most refused, opting to stay and rebuild despite losing eligibility for future relief funding when the next flood strikes.

The relief funding was crucial for those with significant losses, as there has never been such a thing as 'flood insurance' in Canada. The Insurance Bureau of Canada defines a flood as overland-flowing water that enters a home through windows, doors and cracks. Insurance will usually cover damage resulting from a burst pipe, or a leaking roof, or sewage back-up. But Canada remains the only G8 country where homeowners cannot insure their property against overland flooding.

The political debates and arguments were often heated, and no one in the province was without an opinion. Controversies continued for months, as did uncertainty for many affected people across southern Alberta. Though the emergency was over and the clean-up complete, the recovery and rebuilding of the hardest-hit areas continued well into the following year, with long-term impacts on families, communities and the province in general likely to reverberate for years to come.

AFTER GOING TO THE SOUTHLAND Leisure Centre to check on the evacuees of Edwards Place, Lorrie went to stay with her sister until the building could be reoccupied.

There was extensive damage to the infrastructure of Edwards Place, King Tower and Murdoch Manor. Of the three Trinity Place buildings, Murdoch was the hardest hit. The heating and hot water boilers were destroyed in all three buildings. The electrical panels were all damaged, but Murdoch's especially so, requiring many specialized parts to be ordered from the United States. All elevator systems required significant repair. The emergency generators, which are required for occupancy, were destroyed at Murdoch Manor and Edwards Place.

There was much clean-up to be done as well. All refrigerators had to be replaced, as the food inside them had turned to rot without power. The basements needed to be pumped out and cleaned. Residents wouldn't be able to return to Edwards Place and King Tower until mid July, and Murdoch Manor a month later.

Even after the reopenings, heating problems occurred and residents of Edwards Place were given space heaters as a temporary remedy. Dom and Sam both returned to Edwards Place after the flood, where they still reside.

SIX WEEKS AFTER THEY REENTERED their house, Jeremy and Lani received a call about an opening in the Saddlebrook temporary housing community established by the provincial government for displaced residents. They went for an interview, and to see the trailer. It was a small 'jack and jill' suite, normally offered to single workers. There was no kitchen, no temperature control, and the doors didn't lock from the inside. It was hardly a solution for a family with two young children. They spent only one night there.

Jeremy continued staying in High River, working his construction job and working in bits and pieces on their property. Lani remained in Calgary with her family. Soon they found a proper trailer for sale. The man who owned it took a keen interest in the family and their well-being. He was a gas fitter by trade, and he happened to have an extra furnace in a shop. He offered to come install it. When he saw Jeremy's electric pressure washer, he insisted on bringing in a much more powerful one, which they used to clean the entire basement.

This was the beginning of Jeremy's home repair project, a long and tortuous endeavour somewhat quixotic in nature. Frustrated by the endless waiting and uncertainty, he decided to take matters into his own hands. If government wouldn't help him, he'd help himself.

Primarily on his own, with friends pitching in a day's work here and there, Jeremy began to repair the house. In early September, the family moved into the trailer, which both eased the stress and frustrated Jeremy more. With his family close to him, he wasn't able to work as much on the house, which had swelled in importance in his mind. Around this time, he also left his construction job, largely as a result of stress.

The studding in the basement had to be entirely ripped out and rebuilt, as did many of the interior and exterior walls on the main floor. Jeremy was no newcomer to construction, but both the scale of the project and the more complex details were beyond his expertise. He relied on advice and his best judgement.

His mental health was becoming an issue. Jeremy knew there wasn't enough of him for both his family and the house, yet he couldn't let go of the house. If he could save the house, he could save the family. Stopping would be defeat, and defeat was unacceptable.

Lani's application in July for disaster relief aid from the provincial government had gotten them $10,000 within a month. This covered their immediate needs and clean-up, but was far from the full cost of rebuilding large parts of their house. Their insurance company had originally declined them; but after a great deal of negative press regarding the insurance industry's handling of flood victim files, they were reassessed. Despite apparent attempts by the adjustor to find justification for a ruling of overland flooding, Jeremy and Lani were granted coverage for the basement only. These funds, however, did not arrive until December, and it was a struggle until that point, especially without Jeremy's regular income.

Jeremy slugged away at the house at a steady pace. He regularly posted photos of his work on social media, which were shared with family and friends. This awareness of his one-man rebuild no doubt contributed to someone nominating them for a local radio station's Christmas miracle program. A large group of people came with cameras to surprise Jeremy while he was working on the house. The rebuild of the house would be covered by a contractor and other companies who were donating their time and resources. Jeremy's lonely battle was being taken over. Though it was difficult for Jeremy to relinquish the project, they were immensely grateful to have their problems solved.

The miracle, however, was not as advertised. The contractor who performed the work did not do so up to Jeremy and Lani's standards, and the house once again became a source of immense frustration for them. The work was often shoddy and unsupervised, and at times in direct violation of their instructions. After one month, the workers began coming less often, and then not at all. No explanation was offered. The stress, uncertainty, and mental anguish returned. Finally, Jeremy removed the workers' lockbox from the door, barring them from entering.

They heard complaints about the company from other customers. But Jeremy and Lani hadn't sought anyone's help; help had come to them. A meeting with the company management seemed to smooth things over. Jeremy returned to doing most of the work himself while the contractor arranged for help from specialized subcontractors. Though the project moved forward once again, there was precious little clarity. One day, some men arrived with a furnace to install. Neither Jeremy and Lani nor the contractor had any knowledge of who they were, who had hired them, or who was paying for the furnace. The workers had few answers to give. Jeremy and Lani put some money aside in case they wound up with a bill for a furnace down the road.

Jeremy's parents moved to High River, storing their belongings at the semi-renovated house while staying in the trailer with the rest of the family. There is optimism that Jeremy, Lani, Hanna and Mya will be able to move back home by the end of May, eleven months after they fled the water.

———————————

FLORENCE AND KEN BOTH eventually moved south to Crowsnest Pass to stay with Laine and Pat. The fate of Florence's house was a subject of changing opinion amongst her family members. Initially, the hope was to try and salvage the house itself by building a new basement on the same lot and setting it on top. However, the cost of such an endeavour when considered with the scale of the damage and the age of the house was a significant drawback.

It was eventually decided to give the house itself away to a company in exchange for their free removal of it. This spared the family, particularly Florence, from having to watch the house Lyle built be torn down. The company will sell it, and the basement will then be demolished. It is uncertain whether a new house will be built on the lot for Florence and Ken, both of whom still live with Pat and Laine.

THE REMAINING INDIVIDUALS FROM these stories are also continuing their personal pursuits one year after the flood.

Gary still lives at the Salvation Army in downtown Calgary, and his struggles with both his sleep and employment are ongoing.

Steve co-founded an immersive marketing and events company in Calgary. He continues to be deeply involved with the parkour community, both locally and broadly.

Sean completed his master's degree in geology and now works in Houston for a major energy company. He splits his time between Texas and Calgary, and still serves with the Highlanders.

Monica and Brittney's friendship grew after organizing

the Moat together, and they joined forces in Monica's business venture helping women find the resources they need to reach their goals in life and enterprise.

Sohkes completed his emergency medical technician training and hopes to join that field. He lives in Calgary, and continues to work as a firefighter at Siksika First Nation.

Louise remained on medical leave for several months before she was able to return to her regular position as the coordinator of the Siksika crisis unit. With the help of her doctors, her PTSD has become manageable, though she still suffers occasional flashbacks of the trauma of flood victims.

Ritch and Cathy found themselves caught in government bureaucracy as they tried to repair their basement in Bowness. Work started and stopped as the construction requirements to qualify for relief funding changed. They tried to match the uncertainty with patience, and found themselves with a changed outlook on life, taking trips to Mexico and Cuba rather than wait until retirement. The work on the basement continues, but there is no sure timeline for completion.

A few weeks after volunteering on Bow Crescent, Dan and Meera were engaged. They took Ritch up on his offer, and were wed in November at the Al Azhar Shrine Centre in Bowness with many friends and family in attendance, including Ritch and Cathy.

REFERENCES

Foran, Max. *Calgary: An Illustrated History.* Toronto: Lorimer, 1978.

Cormier, Ray. *Inglewood & Ramsay: Cradle of Calgary.* Calgary: Century Calgary Publications, 1975.

Trafford, Tyler. *The Evolution of the Calgary Zoo.* Calgary: Calgary Zoo, 2006.

Bowman, James, and Elspeth Cameron. *Calgary Historical Walking Tour: Mission and Cliff Bungalow.* Calgary: Alberta Community Development, 2001.

Ward, Tom. *Cowtown: An Album of Early Calgary.* Calgary: City of Calgary Electric System, McClelland and Stewart West, 1975.

MacEwan, Grant. 100 *Years of Smoke, Sweat and Tears.* Calgary: Calgary Fire Department, 1984.

McClure, Matt and Trevor Howell. "Forecast Failure: How flood warnings came too late for southern Albertans." *Calgary Herald,* December 27, 2013.

Howell, Trevor. "The untold, tragic story of an Alberta flood victim." *Calgary Herald,* January 6, 2013.

Platt, Michael. "Alberta man killed trying to stem flooding from rampaging Sheep River." *Calgary Sun,* June 24, 2013.

Richards, Gwendolyn. "Two flood victims hailed as heroes." *Calgary Herald,* June 25, 2013.

Platt, Michael. "Family and friends of Calgary's only known flood casualty mourn her loss." *Calgary Sun,* July 2, 2013.

Fortney, Valerie. "Flood at the Zoo: The inside story." *Calgary Herald* http://blogs.calgaryherald.com/2013/11/22/flood-at-the-calgary-zoo-the-inside-story/

Davison, Janet and Lucas Powers. "Why Alberta's floods hit so hard and fast." *CBC* http://www.cbc.ca/news/canada/calgary/why-alberta-s-floods-hit-so-hard-and-fast-1.1328991

"Alberta's flood of floods." Environment Canada http://ec.gc.ca/meteo-weather/default.asp?lang=En&n=5B A5EAFC-1&offset=2&toc=show

Alberta Environment, various maps, data, charts, advisories. http://environment.alberta.ca

"International Energy Statistics." U.S. Energy Information Administration. http://www.eia.gov/cfapps/ipdbproject/IEDIndex3.cfm?tid=5&pid=57&aid=6

"The Impact of Social Media on the Calgary Flood." Inbound Interactive. October 31, 2013. http://www.inboundinteractive.ca/the-impact-of-social-media-on-the-calgary-flood/

Paynter, Paul and Rachel Yin. "Calgary, Canada: A Global Energy and Financial Centre." The World Financial Review: January 2013.

TAYLOR LAMBERT is a Canadian journalist, and the author of *Leaving Moose Jaw*. He has spent a lot of time in a lot of different places, but nowhere so much as Calgary.

Visit tslambert.com